Designing Jewelry with
GLASS BEADS

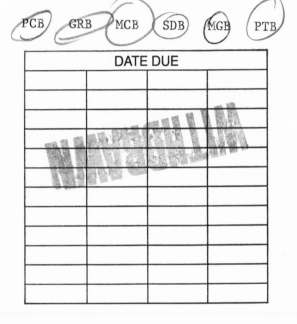

INTERWEAVE PRESS
interweavebooks.com

Photography by Joe Coca
 unless otherwise indicated

Text © 2008 Stephanie Sersich
Photography © 2008 Interweave Press LLC
 except where otherwise noted.
Illustrations © 2008 Interweave Press LLC
Jimi Hendrix Experience image on page
 67 © Bill Graham Archives, LLC/
 www.Wolfgangsvault.com

Interweave Press LLC
201 East Fourth Street
Loveland, CO 80537-5655 USA
interweavebooks.com

Printed in China by Asia Pacific Offset

Library of Congress Cataloging-in-Publication Data

Sersich, Stephanie, 1976-
 Designing jewelry with glass beads / Stephanie Sersich, author.
     p. cm.
 Includes index.
 ISBN-13: 978-1-59668-047-0 (pbk.)
 1. Beadwork. 2. Jewelry making. 3. Glass beads. I. Title.
 TT860.S46 2008
 745.594'2--dc22

                    2007027320

10 9 8 7 6 5 4 3 2 1

[ACKNOWLEDGMENTS]

MY PARENTS AND MY BROTHER, JOHN, have always been an endless source of inspiration and good humor for me. I am grateful for their constant encouragement and love. Tom and Ivory, thank you both so much for supporting all of my wild and crazy endeavors. Interweave Press has made this book a beautiful reality thanks to the patience and efforts of Anne Merrow, Jamie Hogsett, and Ann Swanson. I greatly appreciate Lauren Hayden's years of making beautiful little beads for me to use in my work and this book. Tom Holland and Kate Fowle—thanks for the use of your amazing bead collection. And I love you crazy bead-people—Sage, Kim and Terry, Libby, Portia, Marge, Sharon, Lori, and my other talented friends who have contributed to the spirit of *Designing Jewelry with Glass Beads*.

[Contents]

Projects   30

Living with Glass and Beads

I can't remember a day without beads. As a little girl, I painted elbow macaroni and ziti and strung it on yarn. When I wanted to be a fairy princess or a mermaid, I would string a necklace before making the other parts of my costumes. Although I didn't have many glass beads then, I had plastic beads, sequins and feathers, charms and washers. Over time, my collection of items-with-holes grew to include shells and glass beads. Even when I learned to make glass beads at age nineteen, I didn't stop collecting and using all kinds of beads in the jewelry I made.

Glass is the most magical of materials.

Once glass is manufactured, there are countless ways to work it. It can have any color or texture and be opaque or translucent. No wonder it's such a popular material for beads.

In working with all types of materials, I've found glass beads the most fun to collect and use because they're diverse and thus versatile. This book is a celebration of glass beads, but as you'll see, I still can't help but use beads made from metal, resin, shell, and everything else to help create the textures and colors of my jewelry. I hope to entice you to work with all materials and to see the possibilities in all kinds of beads.

Glass is the most magical of materials. If you have ever watched a glass-blower or lampworker at her craft—turning solid glass into a molten fiery blob, stretching and shaping a form that looks nothing like the raw materials—you know why I call it magical. It can take on innumerable appearances, looking shiny or matte and all of the lusters between. Like other collections and hobbies, the more you learn about glass beads, the more you can enjoy them. As you learn about the processes and origins of glass beads, your own collection will almost certainly grow. You'll also find that your knowledge and enthusiasm will make your jewelry creations more meaningful.

[WHAT IS GLASS?]

Although glass is a unique and distinct material, it has basic raw ingredients—sand, potash (potassium carbonate), and the mineral lime. It takes on color when metallic oxides and minerals are added to the basic ingredients. From a scientific perspective, glass is unclassifiable and therefore mystifying. You may have heard glass referred to as a "super-cooled liquid," because at room temperature it moves so slowly that it is considered a solid. That may sound crazy, and it's why some find glass so alluring: No one knew how to classify it for many years because it has no definite melting or freezing point and no crystalline structure like a mineral or gemstone. Its random atomic structure makes glass versatile enough to take on almost any shape, texture, or color.

It is important to separate the manufacture of glass itself from glass-working. Making glass from raw materials is *primary* glasswork. *Secondary* glasswork is the manufacture of finished pieces from glass stock like rods, sheets, or *cullet* (small pellets that are melted in a furnace). Once glass is manufactured, there are countless ways to work it. While it's hot, one can mold or press it, extrude it, work it in a flame, fuse it, and slump it. In its cold state, it can be cut, crushed, ground, polished, etched, or treated with sparkly finishes. It can have any color or texture and be opaque or translucent. No wonder it's such a popular material for beads.

The ways in which glass is worked to make beads helps us to identify where and when a bead was made. Some methods are popular worldwide, while others are only used by certain beadmakers or regions. There is a world of glass beads out there!

[INSPIRATION]

Each person's individual preferences and artistic inspirations evolve from our unique, personal environment. I grew up with a mom who loves ethnic art and talismans and a dad who likes to keep things organized. My jewelry visually reflects that combination of characteristics, though that isn't to say that all of the aspects of my artistic voice are derivative of their traits. (I love candy-colors and glitter, which my mom could do without.)

An artistic voice evolves from many combined attributes and preferences that are manifested in a unique vision. Personal, identifiable influences draw me to an artist's work. The original inspiration is recognizable but altered enough to create a new and separate revelation. I'm also attracted to the great technical skill in their media that has allowed artists to realize their visions.

Interspersed among the projects, I've highlighted the work of a few artists working in glass bead jewelry (among other media) and asked them to share the ideas or images that inspired a particular piece. Looking at the inspiration and finished artwork side by side hints at the creative spark at work. Other sidebars give a look inside my own artistic process; as a lampwork artist, I make many of the glass beads in my jewelry and design some components. As you discover your own inspirations and artistic preferences through the projects, see the ways that others convert their ideas into artwork.

Glass Beads through the Ages

The history of the beads I've acquired gives me a feeling of connection to the people who made and wore them before me. Throughout history, beads have conveyed status and wealth; they have been used extensively for trade. Culturally, beads have signified protection, religion, and remembrance. Beads are so historically significant and distinctive that they are used as an archeological tool to date other artifacts, revealing manufacturing processes in specific regions and at specific times in human history.

[ANCIENT GLASS BEADS]

As early as the fourth millennium BCE, the Egyptians used glazed silicate called "faience," a precursor to glass. They made beads that were substituted for precious and semiprecious stones.

The origin of glass beads is the origin of glass itself—the earliest man-made glass items were beads. Evidence from Syria and Mesopotamia suggests that beads were wound from glass before 2000 BCE (see page 19 for more on wound beads). After 1400 BCE, the New Kingdom in Egypt supported a beadmaking industry, with royalty employing jewelers and beadmakers. The glassworkers formed guilds, making large numbers of glass beads and core-vessels (small pots built around a clay core or armature). At first, the beads were decorated with simple wavy lines, but by the Amarna period at the height of the New Kingdom, beadmakers produced miniature master-pieces. They made beads from cross-sections of complex drawn cane, combining earlier processes to create beads with phenomenal detail.

In the first millennium BCE, newly established Mediterranean colonies made original beads for the growing international trade. Beads from this time are characterized by a stratified-eye design in blue, white, and yellow colors. Small figurative pendants of birds, animals, and human heads were attributed to the glass beadmakers of Carthage and Phoenicia (now Lebanon). Glassworking secrets then spread to North Africa, the Black Sea, and Indo-European tribes.

A VARIETY OF ANCIENT AND HISTORIC BEADS FROM THE FIRST MILLENNIUM BCE TO ABOUT 1400 CE

PHOENECIAN BEAD

CHINESE WARRING
STATES BEAD

HELLENISTIC-ERA
MEDITERRANEAN BEADS

ROMAN CHECKERBOARD CANE
BEAD AND MOSAIC FACE CANE
BEAD

STRING OF ROMAN
COBALT BEADS

By the time of the Warring States Period (473–256 BCE), the Chinese were producing their own glass beads. Some historians believe that the Chinese discovered glassworking independently. Chinese beads emphasized surface decoration and were the most intricate dotting patterns to date. Stratified-eye beads from this period are some of the most complex and exact in history—especially amazing considering the primitive furnace and tools used to assemble them.

Mediterranean glass beadmakers of the Hellenistic era (331–64 BCE) developed several significant techniques still in use today. Cut and layered glass was used to make beads that resembled banded agate. They also pioneered the use of gold foil with glass, a combination popular throughout art history.

Romans of the Imperial period (27 BCE–610 CE) were extensive travelers and traders, and their empire included places as distant as Switzerland, England, and Egypt. Beadmakers and other craftspeople migrated to Rome and set up factories. There the industry thrived because of faster, more precise processes. The intricacies of the "mosaic face cane" and tiny checkerboard designs on beads from this era make them collector favorites. Glassblowing was also conceived, allowing the glassworker to draw out hollow, tube-shaped beads.

Glass beadmaking was intriguing and profitable. Raw glass was traded as ingots (patties), allowing beads to be made where glass itself wasn't. Primary and secondary glassworking facilities were separate industries in the ancient world as they are today. Secondary manufacturers multiplied, all importing glass from primary sources around the Mediterranean. Primary glassmaking industries, in Egypt and Israel, were far from population centers.

They supplied glass to the western beadmaking industries, which had already been scattered in Europe and were now spreading to the north and east. Southeast Asia began experimenting with secondary glass techniques, making both wound and drawn beads.

Beads have had a talismanic purpose throughout Southeast Asia, making them a valuable commodity even when the supply is bountiful. Glass beads are particularly desirable because of their durability. Objects and costumes are decorated with glass beads to symbolically convey strength and protection. Glass seed beads have come from Indian trade since the first century and have been used for weaving and embroidery in Indonesia ever since.

Beadmaking thrived in India from the beginning of the Common Era until the 1400s. By trading its valuable spices and other dry goods including beads, India became a strong link to Southeast Asia and the Pacific Islands. The drawn "Indo-Pacific" trade bead was born in the first century CE in southern India and is said to be the most widely traded bead in history, found from the Pacific Islands to southern Africa. Indonesians—specifically beadmakers from East Java—made large and bold interpretations with mosaic millefiori, known as Jatim beads, which are still created to this day.

From 700–1400 CE, Arab and Islamic cultures dominated trade. The Muslim world, centered in Baghdad, cultivated fine crafts that were distinctively Islamic and established the last phase of ancient glasswork. They made mosaic beads like their predecessors, but they also developed Fustat and folded beads, the latter having leaf-shaped patterns created by overlapped ridges. Because Islamic art avoids actual representation of the divine in favor of the abstract and symbolic, patterns on Islamic beads were simple and geometric.

ABOVE, SMALL MULTICOLORED INDO-PACIFIC BEADS AND LARGER GREEN DRAWN BEADS FROM THE SAME ERA

JATIM BEAD

FOLDED BEADS

FUSTAT BEADS

VENETIAN
LAMPWORKED BEADS

BOHEMIAN
PRESSED BEADS

[MODERN GLASS BEADS]

During the fifteenth century, the Renaissance, and throughout the 1800s, Venetians produced glass beads that were sold and traded all over the world. In 1292, the island of Murano was established as both a primary and secondary glass-manufacturing center; glass-workers were confined there because industrial fires were common and their techniques were secret. Around 1500, drawn beads were reinvented and improved by the new Italian technology. The bead market demanded a more expensive art bead, and the Murano arti-sans met the challenge with the lamp-wound bead, or "lampworked bead" as we now know it. (The exact origin of lampworking is disputed, but illustrations from the Renaissance period show beads being made over a torch fueled by gas and oxygen.) These beads were time-consuming, made one at a time over an oil lamp powered with oxygen pumped by a foot pedal. By 1602, there were 251 bead-making companies in Venice.

Tradesmen of Bohemia and Moravia (now the Czech Republic) learned the Venetians' glass and beadmaking secrets in the seventeenth century and started their own factories. The hardwood forests of Eastern Europe provided fuel for the furnaces, and the industry flour-ished. At first their beads were mostly copies of Venetian beads, but they began making blown and mandrel-pressed beads of their own design and innovation. Glassblowing and flameworking centers like Lauscha, Germany, cultivated a glassworking tradition that continues today.

Other Europeans, including the Germans and Dutch, made beads that were traded to the New World by the Dutch East India Company. Ironically, the glass beads made during the European expansion weren't worn by Europeans, who preferred precious metals and gemstones. Beads were trinkets, made specifically for trade. The foreign markets were vast, and explorers, traders, and missionaries carried beads for gifts and trade.

Glass beads had arrived in Africa in the seventh century, when Muslims conquered Mediterranean Africa and traded cloth and beads for gold, ivory, and slaves. Around 1500, powerful West African states began a trade with Europe that lasted for centuries. Drawn seed beads and Venetian glass were popular with Africans, who loved color. In almost every part of Africa, beads were essential for personal adornment. In North Africa, the Berbers and other nomadic tribes created unique headdresses and necklaces by assembling all sorts of beads and fibers—amber, glass, silver, wood, and coral—into their signature colorful and asymmetrical jewelry. Beads were worn not only for beauty but to convey familial affiliations, age, marital status, and wealth. In Yoruba and Ndebele tribes, intricate seed bead patterns and sculptural beadwork were made into totemic structures and crowns. Beads decorated the ritual costumes of many African nations.

The story of glass beads in America is relatively short. In 1492, Columbus imported the first glass beads. They were colorful, shiny, hard, and durable—qualities prized by Native Americans. They began integrating seed bead work in place of their traditional quillwork. Over the next several centuries, explorers from England, France, Sweden, Holland, and Spain traveled to North America with ships full of beads to trade for furs, gold, and other riches. European motifs as well as materials began to influence the traditional beadwork.

Important developments in Western jewelry design were made in the late nineteenth century, when the Arts and Crafts movement brought a resurgence of handmade art. Exhibitions of handcrafted furniture, rugs, pottery, and jewelry were popular, and craftsmen and women were appreciated and supported by the elite. In the art nouveau period that followed, style, design, and individual creativity were more highly valued than the preciousness of the materials. The art deco era of the 1920s and 1930s made big, beaded costume jewelry popular.

CORAL, SILVER, TURQUOISE, AND GLASS BEADS ADORN A BERBER NECKLACE

The world of glass beads unites admirers, collectors, designers, consumers, creators, and researchers.

Jewelry design icon Miriam Haskell helped inspire others to make ornate jewelry with simple yet elegant materials. Her classic designs are infused with the desire for creativity and individuality, matching the American woman's psyche. The 1940s made charm bracelets and large cocktail rings all the rage, and more designers started to make bold jewelry in the 1950s. The oppression of the war gave way to a new attitude about life and style. There were fewer restrictions and more individualism. Fashion was fun and for everyone, instead of reserved for the wealthy. In the 1960s, beads were everywhere, a hip symbol of love and freedom of expression. During this time there was no significant glass beadmaking in the United States, though as early as the 1940s immigrants were lampworking as part of sideshows at carnivals.

The Studio Glass Movement took glassmaking from sideshow to center stage. Although there are thousands of glass beadmakers working in North America today, the Studio Glass Movement is newer than you might think. Although glassblowing became an American studio art in the late 1950s, the Corning Museum of Glass held the first official international exhibition for lampworkers in the 1970s, inspiring new artists and celebrating the pioneers. While there had been a few books on the subject, the first lampworking workshop only took place in 1983, at Pilchuck Glass School. A few bead lovers who tried making beads like the ancients were the foundation for the International Society of Glass Beadmakers (ISGB), established in 1993.

MIRIAM HASKELL
EARRINGS

CLOCKWISE FROM LEFT, BEADS BY KATE FOWLE-MELENY, SAGE HOLLAND, KRISTINA LOGAN, AND TOM HOLLAND BLEND ANCIENT INFLUENCES WITH MODERN TECHNOLOGY.

They combined their research into the historical techniques with new lampworking technology. They gathered in Prescott, Arizona, when the Bead Museum hosted an exhibition of their work in 1993.

Today, there are thriving beadmaking industries in China, India, Indonesia, Africa, Germany, and the Czech Republic, all of which grew from the pioneers that preceded them. The beads made in these huge production facilities are primarily for export; the West consumes most of the glass beads produced in the rest of the world. Although Japan and Murano have their own niche markets, the United States dominates the one-of-a-kind art-glass bead market. Its glass beadmakers work in private studios and satisfy an avid following who support their time-consuming creations.

Today, we have bead societies and marketplaces exclusively devoted to glass beads. The world of glass beads unites admirers, collectors, designers, consumers, creators, and researchers. Honoring the history and symbolism of glass beads throughout the world can help you shape new ideas and give you the confidence to be part of the evolution of glass bead jewelry.

ABOVE LEFT, TWO BLOWN-GLASS BEADS BY HAROLD COONEY; ABOVE RIGHT, TWO CONTEMPORARY ITALIAN BLOWN-GLASS BEADS

ABOVE, VENETIAN "WATERMELON" BEADS; BELOW, CONTEMPORARY DRAWN-GLASS BEADS BY LINDA PERRIN

[MAKING GLASS BEADS]

Today's glass beadmakers draw on techniques and traditions from all over the world to create unique effects. From inexpensive seed beads to handmade works of art, the range of glass beads available today is unprecedented—beyond the wildest dreams of our beadmaking ancestors. Each kind has a distinct beauty, and selecting a variety will give added dimensions to your pieces.

Blown-glass beads are made over a torch and formed by inflating a molten ball on the end of a tube, sometimes into a mold but often free-hand. They are traditionally made in Italy. This is a popular technique for contemporary beadmakers working in borosilicate (hard) glass.

Drawn or furnace beads are made through the ancient process of pulling a *gather* (molten mass) of glass into a tube and slicing the drawn cane to make beads. Chevrons, white hearts, and seed beads are all types of drawn beads. This technique can be used to create many looks. In India and Italy, drawn beads are brightly colored and often melon or tube-shaped. Furnace glass beads are popular contemporary drawn beads. Patterned drawn beads are easy to identify because their decoration runs parallel to the perforation (hole).

] CHEVRON BEADS [are a distinctive type of drawn bead formed of consecutive layers made over a star-shaped molded core. The glass is heated and drawn, then cooled and shaped on a grinding machine. Made in Venice since 1500 and heavily traded in Africa, the classic white, blue, and red chevron beads are perhaps the most famous glass beads. Today, small chevrons are drawn in India and China. Contemporary glassworkers in the United States and Italy also make meticulously crafted chevrons.

] SEED BEAD [is the generic term for any small uniformly shaped round or cylindrical bead. They are mechanically drawn, made by a machine that forms a bead from a softened glass rod and a steel die stamp. Seed beads are popular all over the world for weaving and stitching patterns, and they make exceptionally good accents when used with other focal beads. Sizes range from 24° (smallest) to 3° (largest). Most seed beads are made in Japan or the Czech Republic, and there are many specific types of seed beads: Delicas or cylinder beads, which are very uniform; bugle beads, which are much longer than standard seed beads; and charlottes, seed beads with one side flattened or faceted for sparkle.

ABOVE LEFT, A TRADITIONAL CHEVRON BEAD; ABOVE RIGHT, THREE CONTEMPORARY CHEVRON BEADS BY HERON GLASS

Wound glass beads are made with the most ancient of glass bead-making techniques: extracting glass from a furnace or other molten source and winding it onto a mandrel. In India and Africa, wound beads are still made the traditional way, by using molten glass taken directly from the crucible in the furnace. Large, chunky beads are wound from melted glass bottles.

CONTEMPORARY TRADITIONAL-STYLE WOUND BEADS

] LAMPWORKED BEADS [are wound beads made by melting glass rods and working them over a torch. Most lampworked beads are made individually on a steel wire called a *mandrel*, which creates the hole in the bead. Several of today's thriving beadmaking industries use lampwork techniques originally developed in Italy. The South Pacific island of Java is known for its beautifully detailed high-quality lampworked beads. Contemporary lampworked beads from China and India are readily available and inexpensive, but they are of significantly lower quality. The contemporary art glass bead movement, centered on lampworked beadmaking, is alive and very well in the United States, and the ancient art has also resurfaced in Japan as well. Lampworked beadmaking is becoming a popular hobby all over the world.

ABOVE LEFT, LAMPWORKED BEAD BY HEATHER TRIMLETT; ABOVE RIGHT, JAVANESE LAMPWORKED BEADS

ABOVE LEFT, VINTAGE VENETIAN MILLEFIORI BEADS; ABOVE RIGHT, A CONTEMPORARY MOSAIC BEAD BY ISIS RAY

] MOSAIC OR MURRINI BEADS [are both drawn *and* wound. "Murrini" glass canes, produced to be sliced and viewed from the end, are heated and applied to plain wound cores or directly to the mandrel. These have been made through most of the Common Era, or over 2,000 years. Ancient Roman face cane beads and vintage Venetian millefiori ("thousand flowers") beads are especially collectible. Several North American and many Japanese beadmakers make contemporary mosaic beads.

Pressed beads are popular, affordable, and simple machine-molded beads. Both vintage and new Czech glass beads are of high quality. Czech pressed beads are the most versatile and useful of all accent beads, and there is an endless variety of shapes and colors. Finishes on pressed beads can be shiny, matte, luster, aurora borealis (AB), or iris. One variety of Czech pressed beads are the "Mali wedding" pendants traded to Africa, which are larger than most Czech glass beads. They come in bright colors, sometimes striped, and are usually drop or tooth shaped. Some special sources have vintage German pressed-glass beads. Because of that country's niche marble-making industry, there are many unique shapes and colors.

ABOVE, MALI WEDDING BEADS; BELOW, CONTEMPORARY AND VINTAGE PRESSED-GLASS BEADS

Cast- or powdered-glass beads are very popular with jewelry designers. Made predominantly in Ghana, West Africa, these are produced by pounding glass from sources such as Coke and beer bottles into a powder, then firing them in a mold. Another type of African powdered-glass bead—one considerably more prized—is a Kiffa bead. Made in Mauritania, these beads are created by women who pulverize recycled glass and seed beads to make colored powder, then mold it into fanciful red, royal blue, and yellow beads, often triangular in shape. A few contemporary artists use *pâte de verre*, a more refined casting technique.

Crystals or cut beads are made from cut and faceted glass. The most common and well-known are from the Swarovski factory in Austria, one of the largest bead and glass factories in the world. Daniel Swarovski refined crystal and developed a machine to cut it, and the crystal that bears his name is said to be the best cut in the world. Although crystals are technically glass beads, few jewelry designers think of them as such.

SWAROVSKI CRYSTAL BEADS

Contemporary art glass beads may be fused, cast, blown, drawn, or coldworked, but they are usually lampworked. The term "art glass beads" refers to those made by craftspeople in small studios. They are highly collectible, individually styled, and can be pricey.

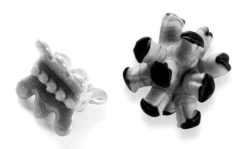

ART GLASS BEADS BY MICHELE
GOLDSTEIN AND AMY JOHNSON

STEPHANIE SERSICH

STEPHANIE SERSICH

Elements of Design

Making art is a combination of practical considerations and creative risks. It is organizing
chaos with flair, relating to a viewer through one
isolated sense. It's a demanding and confusing
process and it's especially difficult to know
where to start.

I have studied my bead collection. When designing, I think of each
item in terms of its usefulness as a material for making jewelry. There
are focal beads, with complex motifs or appealing surfaces, and
those are interesting enough that they can be strung with just a few
other accent beads. There are other beads that are dainty and a little
bit reflective, and those may need to be used with beads that give
them more sparkle. I am familiar with what I have, so I can always be
looking for what I don't. I collect by filling in the holes in my collection. I want a type of bead for every stringing and stitching situation.

I like to think of beaded jewelry as a wearable collection or a
revolving display. When I string beads, I choose what to put where
and how to present it. I think about how to best showcase my fabu-
lous collection of beads. I bunch them up in certain ways to make
the presentation just right. I leave other sections simple so the focal
points stand out. Every element is important. I put colors next to
one another that make my socks go up and down . . . salmon and
chartreuse, yum!

Beading is a miniature game of organizing space. It's compartmen-
talizing, aligning, balancing, and arranging. I like to sort and keep
order—I get it from my Dad. I enjoy making something recognizable
from chaos. I like to try combinations of elements and decide which
are the best.

MY PARENTS' DRESSING ROOM AND
PANTRY SHOWCASE THEIR BEAUTIFUL
JUMBLED COLLECTIONS.

I grew up among collections. My parents' home is full of them, and none are in drawers. They fill big bowls on tables, hang on upholstered walls, and nestle on out-of-the-way shelves. It's a personal museum for the precious items gathered in a shared lifetime. In my own home, there are several vignettes, places I have organized with displays of various little groups of objects: Goofy hats hang on a line of hooks in my bedroom. Strands of lampworked beads made by artists around the world glow in my sunny dining room windows. Miniature ceramic and glass vessels march along the top of a doorframe.

Growing up among my family's organized collections of marvelous stuff gave me a desire to create jewelry with the same feeling. Each piece I make is an arrangement of my design, made from my collected and selected components.

Whether it's music, visual art, or poetry, artists have basic principles that help shape the best creations and make them expressive and aesthetically pleasing. While a beautiful piece of art may seem like an organic piece that sprang fully formed from the artist's hands, there are a few basic concepts that help get the process of creation started or guide it in a constructive way. These ideas are not rules, but the words can help us talk about design, in jewelry or any other art form. Keep them in mind and see if they help make your own jewelry designs more successful.

Beading is a miniature game of organizing space.

ANNE LENOX

CRAB PAGODA

[REPETITION]

Repeating a color or motif yields a cohesive piece with its own rhythm. When one's eye sees more than one of something, the brain wants to make sense of it and creates a rhythm of strong and weak elements. Visual patterns are easy to organize and make an object pleasing to view—think of a pod of peas, a bed of flowers, or a city skyline. Try making every third bead in your design the same color or repeating one shape at different points in the same necklace.

On the other hand, beware of patterns and designs that look canned or predictable. Strive to create a recognizable pattern with unique items, and that pattern will become the "glue" that holds the elements together.

My mom made the crab pagoda sculpture on Star Island, one of the Isles of Shoals located off the coast of Maine and New Hampshire. It is the result of a few days of collecting. I love the way that she has given the collection a new life that celebrates their previous purposes as dwellings.

The bauble necklace is another example of a collection displayed in a repetitive pattern. I used all round beads and positioned the beads in a graduated shape. This creates harmony, so that the beads can all be different from one another and still have a cohesive effect.

BAUBLE NECKLACE

[BALANCE]

Look around—we're surrounded by balance. Mother Nature creates a balance between and within living things. It's an instinctive preference that helps to achieve stability and control. Think of the natural balance of the shape of a flower, tree, or a winged creature. Just as ancient architects did, modern engineers design buildings that rely on symmetry and balance for function and beauty. On a metaphorical level, we each strive to balance our lives to achieve optimal health and happiness.

In jewelry design, we consider both visual and physical balance. Symmetry is one way jewelry designers create balance. Creating physical balance helps a piece of jewelry drape or hang well on the wearer. For instance, a designer should consider a large, heavy item in the center of a long necklace, or the clasp will move around to the front after several minutes of wear.

We love the shape of hearts, whether they're long and lacy or puffy and voluptuous. As a universal symbol, it holds tremendous meaning; it is strong, but also feminine, and its mirror-image shape is naturally comforting. My mom and I both like to incorporate heart motifs, like this paper valentine she made in 1978 and the symmetrical necklace with a heart-shaped pendant that I made in 2005. The shape is visually balanced and is an ideal motif for creating intimate relations, visual strength, or just positive feelings.

HEART NECKLACE

1978 PAPER VALENTINE

A PIRATE'S
VALENTINE

[CONTRAST]

A little disparity creates interest. Contrast can exist in the colors, shapes, or motifs of a piece, giving it a distinctive mood or feeling. The counterpoint of repetition, contrast is another manifestation of human nature. Something different on the horizon catches our eye; we can't help but be drawn to the runt of the litter, the black sheep, or the boat in the harbor with the bright red hull. Interesting and artful jewelry contains varying elements, too.

Contrast works when the items still live in harmony. If objects are very different in color, shape, material, and motif, usually they just don't go together. For example, you usually want to keep the colors close if the textures or shapes are very different.

The Pirate's Valentine necklace that I made with Michele Goldstein combines both of our beads into a piece that seems a little naughty and a little nice. We made something that reflects the quirkiness we share. Michele's ivory skull beads were the perfect complement to my brightly colored hearts. I like the fact that our beads are very different but seem even more playful when put together.

[TEXTURE]

Dimensional qualities are especially important in jewelry. As a three-dimensional art form, beading can combine countless stitches and formations that are unachievable in other media. The stitches and beads can be tiny and intricate or bulbous and projectile, even within the same piece of jewelry. I feel it is a jewelry designer's duty to experiment with riotous textures. Beads can be combined with fibers, organic materials, and found objects to achieve a desired texture. Textures don't always have to be wild or rough, either; smooth textures can be beautiful and appropriate for particular designs. Using both smooth and rough textures together can create contrast and in turn strengthen an effect.

A little vignette sits in my parents' living room. They've collected funky textured seed balls, beads, and magic items—pitted, hard, sleek and smooth—and displayed them in a corner where they wait to be touched.

I also strive to put together textured displays with tiny items. The branch coral and stacked components give this necklace its texture and personality. Some parts of the necklace are smooth and glassy, others pointed and ridged, still more supple and fibrous. The texture of this piece makes me want to reach out and touch it, a desire to investigate that brings me back to the time when I was a kid picking shells up off the beach.

STEPHANIE SERSICH

TEXTURED VIGNETTE

TREE-SNAIL NECKLACE

STEPHANIE SERSICH

AMSTERDAM FRUIT
MARKET

[COLOR]

Color is relegated to a wheel in many design texts. Although color can be discussed technically and theoretically, and some designers have do's and don'ts, many artists work with color instinctively—their eyes naturally tell them which hues work well together. If you were born without these instincts, you can still train yourself to become tuned in to them. Use everyday objects or themes to get started, keep a few considerations in mind, and you can balance colors in your projects like an artist with a natural sense of color.

This fruit at the flower market in Amsterdam was texturally inspiring—notice the pointy skin on the fruit—but the colors made me squeal with delight. The fruit looked juicy and the colors electric, almost unnatural, but very edible. I wanted to touch the fruits and see if they were really that color and texture. The green pepper necklace was made the day after I printed my photos from the trip.

Experiment with the following methods to create your own rich and balanced color scheme.

] **THINK WITHIN A SCHEME AND THEN ADD A CONTRASTING OR SECONDARY COLOR.** [I like reds and greens together, but they look too much like Christmas if they're the only colors used in a piece. I try adding a little purple, black, white, or even silver to remove the association with a holiday color scheme.

GREEN PEPPER
NECKACE

Even if you find several contrasting or secondary colors that might work, you don't need to use them all. First try using just one secondary color. (The choices you make as a designer have as much to do with what's not included in a piece as what is.) But if the piece still needs pep, try adding a second or third contrasting color as well.

] BASE THE COLORS ON ONE ELEMENT AND BUILD THE OTHER COLORS AROUND IT. [This is what to do when you have special beads that you're excited to use as the focus of a design as in the multistrand starfish necklace. Especially if you've collected each element one at a time and there's variation within the focal pieces, you'll want to create the background that displays the special beads to their best advantage. Choose a background color that best supports the focal beads. Try neutral greens, tans and browns, black, and midnight blue to set the stage for your show-stoppers.

] CHOOSE A MOOD OR THEME. [Finding a theme gives a viewpoint from which to choose materials. I had a "cowgirl wedding" theme in mind for the earrings below. To create that feeling, I used stars, western motifs, silver beads, and arid colors—tans, browns, and sky blue. I made the texture celebratory as well, using elements that stick off like confetti or a tiered skirt.

MULTISTRAND STARFISH NECKLACE

INGREDIENTS FOR A
SPINY KNOTTED
BRACELET

COWGIRL WEDDING
EARRINGS

Think of beaded jewelry as a wearable collection or revolving display.

[The Projects]

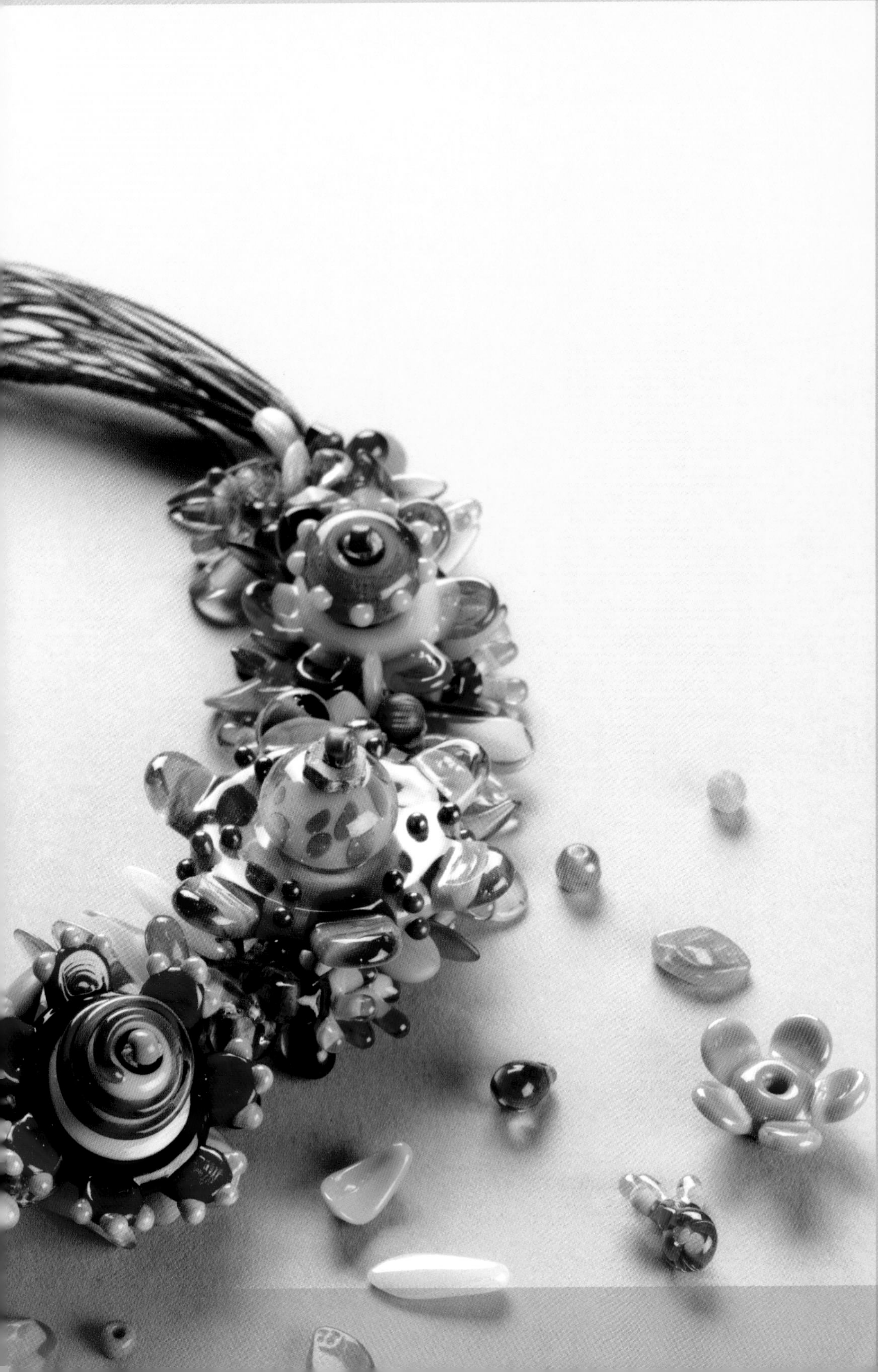

Tinkerbell Drops

These earrings are girly, fun, and easy! The little flower bead "skirt" reminds me of Tinkerbell, Peter Pan's sassy fairy friend.

[CHOOSING BEADS]

These earrings can feature many different shapes and sizes of flowers and beads, as you can see in the variety of samples pictured. Because the earrings are a happy shape, I like to use light or bright colored beads. Light and bright colors also show up well on most shades of hair. Choose focal beads that have a large enough hole that they sit nicely atop the flower.

[DESIGN TIP]

The most basic and useful wirework technique, a wrapped loop is outlined in the glossary of basic techniques (see page 125). Making earrings is a great way to practice those loops. Before making the wrapped loop, make sure all of the beads nestle together well.

MATERIALS

4 size 8° seed beads
2 Czech pressed-glass or Lucite flowers
2 lampworked beads or other focal beads
2 Czech pressed-glass 6mm rondelles
2 head pins
2 ear wires

TOOLS

Round-nose pliers
Wire cutters

FINISHED SIZE

1¼–1¾" (3.2–4.5 cm)

FIGURE 1   FIGURE 2

1 | Use 1 head pin to string 1 seed bead, 1 flower, 1 focal bead, 1 rondelle, and 1 seed bead (**Figure 1**). Form a wrapped loop.

2 | Use the round-nose pliers to open the loop on the ear wire, attach the wrapped loop, and close the ear wire (**Figure 2**). (If using ear wires with soldered loops, attach the head pin to the ear wire before wrapping the loop.)

3 | Repeat Steps 1 and 2 to make the second earring.

The Art of Lampwork
Making a Glass Bead

I make lampworked (also known as flameworked) glass beads. The glass, in the form of a thin rod, is melted over the torch and wound around a steel mandrel (piece of wire) held in the nondominant or "spinning" hand. As long as the bead is kept warm, it can be reformed and manipulated. Spinning the bead helps to keep the bead round and the glass well-distributed on the mandrel.

CAROLYN RAMSAY

The glass rods come in many colors, both opaque and transparent. When I want to add a new color, I heat the tip of another rod and touch it to the bead. I use the hot flame to "cut" the rod of glass away from the bead and then reheat the bead to make sure the new protrusion is well-fused. After I've decorated the bead to my liking, I put it in a hot kiln and then let it cool. The kiln strengthens and then cools the beads slowly so they don't crack apart. After they have been fired and cooled, the beads are removed from the kiln and twisted off their mandrels.

A love of beads is what drew me to the desire to make them, but the versatility of glass is what made beadmaking an obsession. The tiny scale of the decorations allow for tremendous detail. Like painting with watercolors, I can use the transparency of the medium to create new colors. Because the medium's transparency can also be used to create dimension, I can magnify these effects as well. The molten glass is like clay— I can sculpt it in three dimensions, so when building the shape of a bead, I appreciate that the hot glass is malleable. All of the dazzling attributes of glass make lampworking a continuing adventure—there are always new combinations of colors and techniques to try.

Fruit Salad Necklace

I've made this style of necklace for many years. I love using beads from all over the world and mixing in a few of my own. The pitted root beer colored bead in the center is a recycled glass bead from Ghana, and the opaque apple-green bicone is an Indo-Chinese bead, several hundred years old. With so many different colors, the necklace goes with any outfit.

[CHOOSING BEADS]

I've used a few horn and resin beads, but most are glass. Before I knew how to make beads, I used batik bone beads from Kenya that look similar to the large hollow black-and-white patterned beads shown here. Try using only one type of bead with a motif, keeping all the others solid in color. The piece will look cohesive, even though there are many varying elements. Look for large, lightweight beads, because the middle of this necklace is heavy if all the beads are solid glass.

[DESIGN TIP]

When you're stringing the big beads, try using a disc or rondelle between the large round beads. This seems to eliminate any space visible between them and helps the continuity of the piece.

MATERIALS

About 20 round beads or rondelles smaller than 10mm (including 2 with holes large enough to cover crimp tubes)
About 20 round beads or rondelles between 10mm and 25mm
About 10 round beads or rondelles between 25mm and 35mm
1 silver hook-and-eye clasp
2 silver crimp tubes
20" (51 cm) of .024 beading wire

TOOLS

Crimping pliers
Flush cutters

FINISHED SIZE

18¼" (46.5 cm)

FIGURE 1

1 Use one end of the beading wire to string 1 crimp tube and one half of the clasp. Pass back through the tube, crimp, and trim wire end. String 1 small large-hole bead to cover the crimp tube, then string half of the smallest beads and rondelles in order from smallest to largest **(Figure 1)**.

2 String half of the medium-size beads and rondelles, adding them in order from smallest to largest. String the largest beads, working from smallest to largest to smallest again, with the largest bead at the middle of the finished necklace. Use rondelles between the larger beads to keep the necklace flexible and allow the round beads to hang nicely.

3 String the remaining beads in reverse order, from largest to smallest. String 1 small large-hole bead as the last bead, then string the crimp bead and the second half of the clasp. Pass back through the tube, snug the beads, and crimp the tube. Trim the wire end.

Gail Crosman-Moore

Borosilicate glass beads and handmade felt jewelry

Gail works in many media, and her work is so organic that it changes with the seasons. Whether it's felt or glass, large or small, the distinctive forms and colors of her work are clearly products of the same style and artistry. She always has some new creation, born or regenerated in her style. Somehow each new item belongs with the rest of her family of creations, even if the material or surface is different. Her style comes through in any material.

GAIL CROSMAN-MOORE

Horticulture and growing up by the sea have given me a wealth of inspiration as well as a vocabulary of form, color, and texture that I rely on in my art-making. These ingredients shape how I see everyday life and the interconnectedness of nature to man.

The focus of my work today is on molten glass and its ability to transmit the light and forms in my mind. Using borosilicate glass offers me the pleasure and surprise of never making the same thing twice. Even if I try to duplicate form, the ratio of propane to oxygen alters the surface in unpredictable ways, as do time in the flame and temperature and time in the annealer. I often include handmade felt in juxtaposition to my glasswork. It is the contrast of surface that engages me, the hard to soft, shiny to matte, cool to warm that keeps this lively dance exciting.

—Gail Crosman-Moore

Funky Fiber Earrings

I often look for an occasion to wear outrageous earrings. I love working with waxed linen, and these earrings complement my knotted bracelets and necklaces. As in the knotted pieces, texture is important. My examples have long, round, disc and star shapes, accented by two sizes of seed beads. All the variation attracts fascination.

[CHOOSING BEADS]

There's no need to follow the materials list exactly. As long as you have some dagger beads and your other beads vary in size and shape, you don't need to have the same Czech druks and rondelles that I used.

[DESIGN TIP]

To give your earrings more texture, use a lot of different shapes of beads. To make them fuller and fluffier, tie the knots and beads closer together. Try different combinations. It's just string—if you don't like how they're turning out, you can just cut the earrings apart.

MATERIALS

8 size 8° seed beads
4 size 6° seed beads
2 lampworked beads or other focal beads
4 6–8mm discs with large holes
6 Czech daggers, teeth, or other top-drilled beads
8 beads in assorted shapes, sizes, and colors
2 ear wires
6' (1.8 m) of 4-ply waxed linen

TOOLS

Scissors

FINISHED SIZE

3¾" (9.5 cm)

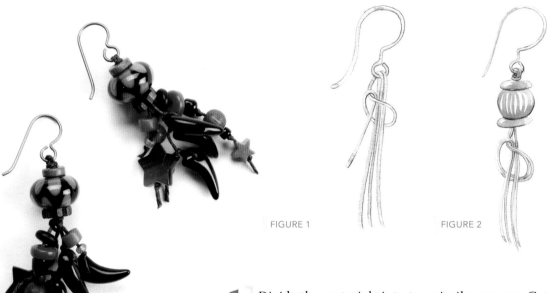

FIGURE 1   FIGURE 2

1 | Divide the materials into two similar groups. Cut the waxed linen into four equal pieces.

2 | Rub the ends of two pieces of the waxed linen together. The ends will stick together slightly, making it easier to string beads. Use the two pieces to string 1 ear wire. Fold the strands in half around the wire. Use one strand of the linen to form a fringe knot around the other three strands, fitting the knot tightly against the ear wire **(Figure 1)**.

3 | Use all four strands of linen to string 1 large-hole disc bead, 1 focal bead, and 1 large-hole disc bead. Snug the beads and use two strands of linen to form a fringe knot around the other two strands, tightly against the bottom disc **(Figure 2)**. This will make a larger knot to prevent the disc from slipping over the knot.

FIGURE 3   FIGURE 4   FIGURE 5   FIGURE 6

4 Use one strand to string 1 dagger. Form a fringe knot
to secure the dagger on a loop of its own, ¼" (6 mm)
from the knot formed in Step 3 **(Figure 3)**. The knot should
be snug against the dagger bead **(Figure 4)**. Repeat two more
times, placing each knot ¼" (6 mm) from the previous knot.
Use the tail thread to string 1 size 8° seed bead, placing
it ¼" (6 mm) from the bottom dagger, and make an overhand knot below it. Trim the tail to ¼" (6 mm) **(Figure 5)**.

5 Use the remaining three strands of linen to randomly
string the rest of the beads, tying knots between some
of the groupings and making varying lengths of strung beads.
Each strand should end with an overhand knot and a ¼" (6 mm)
tail **(Figure 6)**.

Wispy Necklace

I love to poke through my mom's eclectic jewelry collection, which contains examples of how beads were used all over the world. Her necklaces from Africa, India, and the Pacific Islands have protrusions that make them texturally scrumptious! I've affection-ately coined the terms "stickey-outey" and "hangey-offey" for protrusions in jewelry.

[CHOOSING BEADS]

The beads used for the dangling wispy "units" have to accommodate two strands of linen. Each unit is made individually. Small lampworked tubes and drawn beads work best because of their large holes.

[DESIGN TIPS]

* Keep the combinations of beads and waxed linen consistent in order to have a cohesive-looking finished piece. For example, every time I make a split unit with red barrels, I use black waxed linen.
* If you begin to string the units and the piece doesn't look full, try stringing smaller beads between the units.

MATERIALS

About 60 size 8° seed beads in each of 2 colors (A and B)

About 50 size 6° seed beads in each of 4 colors (C, D, E, and F)

About 50 disc-shaped 4–6mm beads in each of 2 colors, including 2–4 beads with holes large enough to cover crimp tubes

About 25 barrel-shaped 10–16 mm long beads in each of 2–3 colors

25 round 8–12mm beads

Silver hook-and-eye clasp

About 6 yd of 4-ply waxed linen in each of 2–3 colors

4–5' (1.2–1.5 m) of .024 beading wire

4 crimp tubes

TOOLS

Crimping pliers

Flush cutters

Scissors

FINISHED SIZE

19" (48.5 cm)

FIGURE 1

FIGURE 2

1 Cut a 5" (12.5 cm) piece of waxed linen. Fold it in half and tie an overhand knot, forming a small loop. Rub the tips of the ends together until they stick. Use both ends of linen to string 1 size 6° (C) bead, 1 barrel bead, and 1 size 6° (C) bead. Tie another overhand knot just below the size 6° bead to hold the beads in place. Trim tails to ¼" (6 mm) long (**Figure 1**). Repeat entire step to make twenty-two units.

2 To make a second kind of unit, or "split unit," cut a 5" (12.5 cm) piece of waxed linen, fold it in half, and tie an overhand knot, forming a loop. Rub the tips of the ends together until they stick. Use both ends of linen to string 1 size 6° (D) bead. Use one end of linen to string 1 barrel and 1 size 8° (A) bead. Tie a simple knot and trim the tails to ¼" (6 mm). Repeat with the other end of linen (**Figure 2**). Repeat entire step to make twenty-two units.

3 Use 48" of beading wire to string the hook half of the clasp. Center the clasp at the midpoint of the wire. Use both ends of wire to string 1 crimp bead. Crimp the tube. Use both wires to string 2 large-hole beads.

FIGURE 3

4 Use 1 wire to string 5 size 8° (B) beads, 1 size 6° (E) bead, 1 size 6° (F) bead, 1 round, 1 size 6° (F) bead, 1 size 6° (E) bead, and 5 size 8° (B) beads. String 1E, 1 split unit, 1E, 1F, 1 unit, 1 round, 1 unit, 1F, 1E, 1 split unit, 1E, and 3B eleven times **(Figure 3)**. String 2B, 1E, 1F, 1 round, 1F, 1E, 5B, 2 large-hole beads, 1 crimp tube, and the eye half of the clasp. Pass back through the tube and crimp.

5 Use the other wire to string 3B. String 1 disc and 1C six times. String 1 disc and 3B. String 1 disc, 1C, 1 round, and 1C eighteen times. String 1 disc and 3B. String 1 disc and 1C six times. String 1 disc and 3B and pass through the 2 large-hole beads at the eye half of the clasp. String 1 crimp tube and the eye half of the clasp. Pass back through the tube and crimp.

Variation

In the red, blue, and yellow necklace, a single alternative unit is used in place of the units described in Steps 1 and 2.

Cut a 5" (12.5 cm) piece of waxed linen. Fold it in half and tie an overhand knot, forming a small loop. Rub the tips of the ends together until they stick. Use both ends of linen to string 1 size 6° bead, 1 barrel bead, and 1 size 6° bead. Separate the tails and string 1 size 6° bead on each tail. Tie an overhand knot just below the size 6° bead to hold the beads in place. Trim tails to ¼" (6 mm) long. Repeat entire step to produce forty-three alternate units. Follow Steps 3–5 as given at left, substituting the alternate unit wherever a unit is called for.

Wirework Brooch

When I make a bead I love, I want to wear it right away. This is a very quick and simple way to make a brooch from a tube or lozenge-shaped bead or to showcase several smaller beads together. My mom often makes little gifts for friends that showcase her current hobby or obsession. Last year, during the months when she explored big beads and wire, she turned many of my beads from her collection into brooches like these.

[CHOOSING BEADS]

For a focal bead, pick a bead that is lozenge-shaped or a skinny tube that has no protrusions. (Because the bead spins on the wire, protrusions would get caught.) You can also choose to use a few small beads in place of one large focal.

[DESIGN TIP]

Pull the wire firmly against the pliers to create sharp angles and loops but don't squeeze the pliers hard, or you'll mar the wire.

MATERIALS

2 size 6° seed beads
2 6mm rondelles
1 tube or lozenge-shaped
    focal bead
1' (30.5 cm) of sterling silver
    16-gauge soft wire

TOOLS

Jeweler's file
Flush cutters
Round-nose pliers

FINISHED SIZE

2" (5 cm)

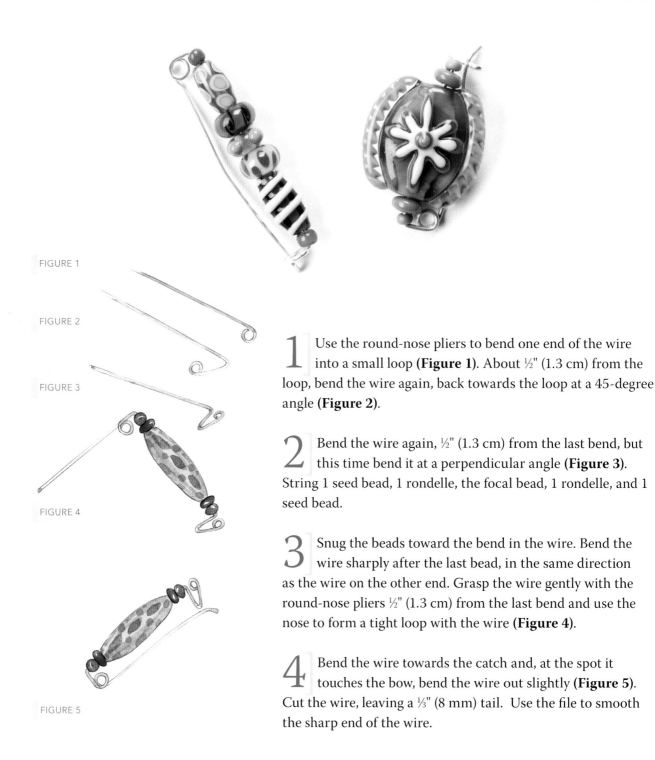

FIGURE 1

FIGURE 2

FIGURE 3

FIGURE 4

FIGURE 5

1 Use the round-nose pliers to bend one end of the wire into a small loop **(Figure 1)**. About ½" (1.3 cm) from the loop, bend the wire again, back towards the loop at a 45-degree angle **(Figure 2)**.

2 Bend the wire again, ½" (1.3 cm) from the last bend, but this time bend it at a perpendicular angle **(Figure 3)**. String 1 seed bead, 1 rondelle, the focal bead, 1 rondelle, and 1 seed bead.

3 Snug the beads toward the bend in the wire. Bend the wire sharply after the last bead, in the same direction as the wire on the other end. Grasp the wire gently with the round-nose pliers ½" (1.3 cm) from the last bend and use the nose to form a tight loop with the wire **(Figure 4)**.

4 Bend the wire towards the catch and, at the spot it touches the bow, bend the wire out slightly **(Figure 5)**. Cut the wire, leaving a ⅓" (8 mm) tail. Use the file to smooth the sharp end of the wire.

Anne Lenox

Talismanic items and jewelry

Anne Lenox is my mom (not to be confused with Annie Lennox, the singer). She creates curiously beautiful things following inspirations from many different sources, from tiny shells to huge rooms. She has been a fashion designer, professional interior designer, feng shui practitioner, college design instructor, knitter, beader, avid cook, and devoted gardener.

I have had two passions since childhood, a fascination with the natural world and with playing "dress-up" and "pretend." My art manifests in costumes, in designing the interiors of houses, or in the magic of my garden. I am empowered by holding stones, seedpods, feathers, sticks and bones, shells, and treasures from the sea in my hands. I want to combine them into wearable art so that other people can experience their own closeness to the earth and its magic.

When I'm creating something, I try to stay in the inquiry/play mode as long as possible, to mix and match, separate and divide, regroup and start again, until I can feel in my gut the combination of items taking on an energy of its own. This is a special zone where judgments and right and wrong do not exist, only the thrill of all the possibilities.

—Anne Lenox

Trapeze Necklace

This necklace is inspired by beaders in Papua New Guinea, who make jewelry that is a harmonious combination of geometric shapes and fibers, using bones, shells, and glass beads. My version puts together these strange shapes in a new way that's a little more wearable. The layout of the shapes in this design creates a pleasing balance. The geometric shapes can be of any size and ratio to one another. Try using a smaller bar or larger rondelle, and they still seem to look balanced.

[CHOOSING BEADS]

Here's another way to hang a disc-shaped bead and see the side of it! Choose a disc, donut, or rondelle that has a smooth perforation so the string doesn't wear on it.

[DESIGN TIPS]

* Wrap the waxed linen as tightly as you can. If you can't get it very tight or you tend to be hard on your jewelry, use a dab of epoxy on the bar before starting to wrap the waxed linen.
* To finish the piece more elegantly, you can tie beads to the ends of the cords.

MATERIALS

16 size 11° seed beads
1 large disc or rondelle
2–3½" (5–8.5 cm) bar
8 Czech pressed-glass 6mm rondelles or beads of a similar size
10' (3 m) of 4-ply waxed linen
26" (66 cm) of cord or ribbon

TOOLS

Scissors

FINISHED SIZE

2 x 2⅓" (5 x 6 cm) pendant

1 | Cut the waxed linen into four pieces, two 3' (1 m) lengths and two 2' (61 cm) lengths.

2 | Hold the midpoints of the bar and cord together. Use the two 3' (1 m) lengths of linen to bind the bar and cord together tightly: Beginning at the middle of the strands of linen, wrap them outward from the midpoints for ¼" (6 mm) in each direction, being careful to keep the strands side by side, then wrap back toward the middle. Secure the ends by tying them in a square knot on the underside of the bar **(Figure 1)**.

3 | Use two of the tail ends of linen from Step 2 and the two 2' (61 cm) lengths of linen to string the disc to about an inch below the bar, placing the midpoints of the 2' (61 cm) lengths of linen at the center of the disc. Use the 2' (61 cm) lengths of linen to tie a fringe knot around all of the tails just above the disc **(Figure 2)**.

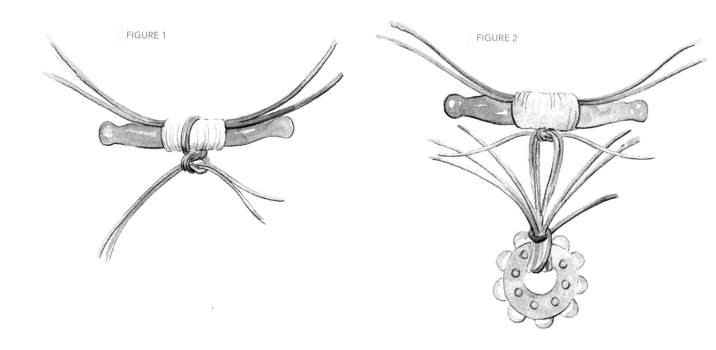

FIGURE 1

FIGURE 2

4 Use one of the remaining tail ends from Step 2 to form tight coils around all of the other strands from the bar down for ½" (1.3 cm). Use one strand from just above the disc to form tight coils around all of the other strands up toward the bar for ½" (1.3 cm). Use this strand and the first strand used in this step to form a square knot on the front of the piece **(Figure 3)**. Use two other remaining strands to form a square knot. Repeat, to tie each strand to another in the center, where they all meet, so there are four square knots altogether.

5 Use one of the tails to tie an overhand knot ¼–½" (6–13 mm) from the square knots. String 1 seed bead, 1 rondelle, and 1 seed bead and tie an overhand knot close to the last bead. Trim, leaving a ¼" (6 mm) tail.

6 Repeat Step 5 for each of the remaining 7 tails **(Figure 4)**.

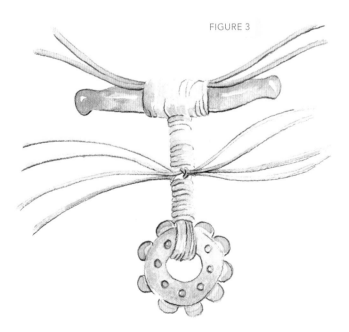

FIGURE 3

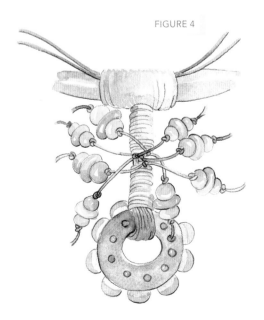

FIGURE 4

Stacked-Bead Pendant

I have a crazy love of Moroccan and Indian tassels—"stickey-outeys" come off all over them. This pendant design is a tribute to those tassels and how happy I get about things that stick out. Creating texture in a piece is most easily achievable when there are no limitations in the materials. In this piece, I use waxed linen and ribbon, jump rings and head pins, and beads to make several different types of attachments. This project is like a recipe that can be adapted to suit a vast array of ingredients. Make sure to add some spice!

[CHOOSING BEADS]

* Experiment with bead shapes to see how they fit into each other. In the large wireworked section, avoid using too many round beads because they don't sit comfortably next to one another. Consider using only one large bead if it has a motif or if the piece begins to look chaotic.

* Almost any bead belongs in this design because the pendant's structure contains such varying elements. This project provides an opportunity to use up leftover beads. Though you could work within a color scheme, try using a random mix. The more choices you have for shapes, the better the outcome.

[DESIGN TIP]

Make large wrapped loops so that you'll be able to change the cords to ones of varying thicknesses, and so you can add dangling pieces at the bottom without worrying how they'll all fit.

MATERIALS

5 size 6° seed beads

8–12 assorted 8–18mm round beads and rondelles

3 pepper or dagger-shaped beads

1 large shell or dangling bead

1 small shell or star bead

3–4 silver 4–7mm jump rings

2 silver head pins

8" (20.5 cm) of sterling silver 18-gauge half-hard wire

2' (61 cm) of waxed 4-ply linen

3' (1 m) of silk ribbon or other cord

TOOLS

Flush cutters

Round-nose pliers

Crimping pliers

Scissors

FINISHED SIZE

4" (10 cm) pendant length

FIGURE 1   FIGURE 2

1 Use the innermost part of the round-nose pliers to form a
large (6mm) wrapped loop on one end of the wire. Trim the
tail of the wire and tuck it in using the crimping pliers **(Figure 1)**.

2 String the round and rondelle-shaped beads on the wire
so that they fit together and remain aligned. (I find that
it works best to gradually increase from small to large to small
again.) Repeat Step 1, using the other end of wire **(Figure 2)**.

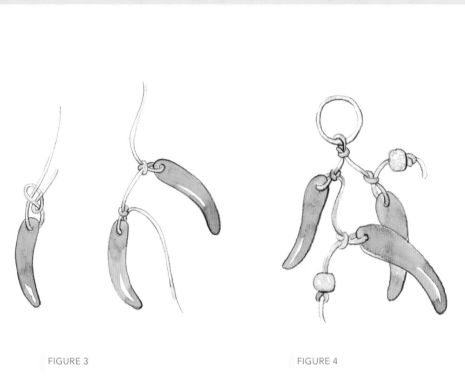

FIGURE 3　　　　　　　　　FIGURE 4

3 Connect the smaller dangly pieces (like peppers and daggers) using the jump rings and waxed linen. To form these parts, simply tie fringe knots above each bead **(Figure 3)**. Tie the waxed linen to a jump ring and continue adding pieces, ending both tails of the waxed linen strand with 1 size 6° seed bead. Tie another overhand knot after each. Trim the linen, leaving a ¼" (6 mm) tail **(Figure 4)**. Attach the jump ring to one of the wrapped loops. Use one or two strands of linen, depending on the size of the hole and the weight of the bead.

4 To attach the larger dangling pieces, open a jump ring, string the bead or wrapped loop, and close the jump ring. (Some beads may need to be made into little pendants. Use the wrapped bail and wrapped-loop techniques on page 125.)

5 String the silk ribbon through the other wrapped loop.

Embellished Ribbon Necklace

In this necklace, I wanted to create a piece where Czech pressed-glass flowers dangled freely on head pins. The rings give them another "hinge" for movement. This feminine piece looks best worn loosely with the ends just tucked around one another. The weight of the glass beads keeps it from coming undone.

[CHOOSING BEADS]

You don't have to use Czech pressed-glass flowers; other glass beads could work, but keep in mind that they must be similar in weight. The beads will clink together when the necklace is worn, so fragile beads are not recommended. Consider the motif when choosing colors. If you're using flowers as I have, keep the colors natural and the ribbon will seem more vinelike.

[DESIGN TIP]

Choose thread and ribbons similar in color or you'll be able to see all of the stitching, inside and out.

MATERIALS

78 assorted size 8° seed beads

39 assorted Czech pressed-glass flowers

39 Czech pressed-glass 8mm rings

39 silver 20- or 22-gauge 1½" head pins with ball end

2 handdyed 40" (101.5 cm) silk ribbons

Size D Nymo beading thread

TOOLS

Round-nose pliers

Flush cutters

Scissors

Size 10 sharp beading needles

Straight pins

Iron

FINISHED SIZE

40" (101.5 cm)

1 Use 1 head pin to string 1 seed bead, 1 flower, and 1 seed bead **(Figure 1)**. Form a wrapped loop that attaches to 1 glass ring, making the loop large enough to move freely around the ring **(Figure 2)**. Repeat to make thirty-nine flower units.

2 Iron the ribbons flat. Use straight pins to pin them together at 2" (5 cm) intervals, lining up the ends.

FIGURE 1   FIGURE 2

3 Use a needle to thread a comfortable length of Nymo. Center the needle on the thread and knot the ends together. Beginning at one end, sew through the ribbons' edges several times. Stitch through a ring of one flower unit and back though the edge of the ribbon (**Figure 3**). Sew through the ring a second time and through the edge again. Whipstitch around the edges for about 1¼" (3.2 cm). Sew through the ring of another flower unit, passing through twice to secure it well. Continue in this manner for the length of the ribbon, placing all thirty-nine flower units. Each time you end the thread, tie the Nymo off inside and start again inside, so the tails are hidden (**Figure 4**).

4 When you reach the other end and sew on the last flower unit, sew the other side without adding any embellishment.

FIGURE 3

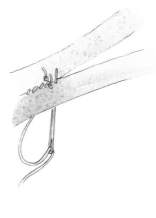

FIGURE 4

Double-Clasp Bracelet

I've always loved objects with interchangeable parts. This piece features two parts, both with clasps made from buttons and simple strung sections, so you can mix and match with odd-size beads. In any project like this where you can use almost any size and shape of bead, make sure to try beads of many shapes and sizes next to one another. Only a few choices will nestle and fit well into the previously strung bead. Stringing projects can take a while because maintaining range of motion in stringing is so difficult to achieve.

[CHOOSING BEADS]

Use small buttons for the clasps. The loops that fit over them will be proportional to the size of the buttons, and you don't want the bracelet to be all loops.

[DESIGN TIP]

Consider weighting the back of the bracelet as you string it by putting heavier beads near one of the buttons.

MATERIALS

About 5 g size 8° seed beads in four colors
35–40 beads in a variety of colors, shapes, and sizes (up to 10 mm), including several rondelles
2 buttons, each about 14 mm
4 crimp tubes
20" (51 cm) of .024 beading wire

TOOLS

Crimping pliers
Round-nose pliers
Flush cutters

FINISHED SIZE

8" (20.5 cm)

Double-Clasp Bracelet

FIGURE 1

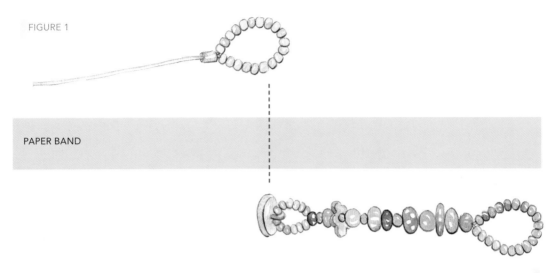

PAPER BAND

FIGURE 2

1 Use 6" (15 cm) of beading wire to string 1 crimp tube and 20 seed beads (or however many will comfortably fit around a button), then pass back through the crimp tube. Snug the beads and tube so that the loop is tight. Test one of the buttons to be sure that is passes through the loop but doesn't slip through too easily. Adjust the number of beads in the loop if necessary. Snug the beads, crimp the tube, and trim the wire **(Figure 1)**.

2 String about 2" (5 cm) of beads as desired; the first and last beads strung should have holes large enough to hide crimp tubes. String 1 crimp bead, 6 seed beads, 1 button, and 6 seed beads. Pass back through the crimp tube and pull the tail tight. Crimp the tube and trim the wire **(Figure 2)**.

3 To determine the desired length of the bracelet, make a paper band for your wrist. Mark the loop and button of the first unit on the band; you will make the second unit as long as the remainder of the paper band.

4 Repeat Steps 1 and 2 to make the second half of the bracelet. Link the two clasps.

Dustin Tabor

Glass beads and jewelry

Dustin's beads are often composed of clear-cased layers of dots, casting shadows of patterns on more patterns below. He uses the overlapping repetitive patterns to create a sense of energy in the bead. While he gets a lot of his natural talent with design and color from his amazing mom, his personal explorations of everything from modern art to ancient artifacts give his work depth and dynamics that set it apart.

Graphic lines, swirling repetitive patterns, and bold colors have always grabbed my attention in a special way. While I find pieces of inspiration from almost everything around me, including textiles, organic forms, and ethnic artifacts, the 1960s and 1970s-era concert posters from venues such as The Fillmore Auditorium and The Avalon Ballroom continue to be my favorite source of inspiration. The influence of the intricate details, the multilayered patterns, and the psychedelic color schemes found on these posters are readily visible in my work.

Glass provides a dynamic medium for me to explore this particular source of inspiration. Like so few other media can, glass is able to capture the movement and texture of a pattern as it emerges from the surface. Couple this rare characteristic with glass's ability to capture and transmit light, and the possibilities are endless.

Spinning-Bead Pendant

I love things that move—carousels, mobiles, and wind chimes. The kinetic jewelry pieces I make are my favorites to wear. The wirework in this project provides an axis on which the big disc or rondelle can spin. Discs and rondelles have radial symmetry, like flower blossoms, stars, and wheels. Radial motifs have been used in many cultures to signify life cycles and unity.

[CHOOSING BEADS]

This pendant provides an opportunity to showcase a favorite lamp-worked disc-shaped bead. Choose a disc that has a detailed motif on the side.

[DESIGN TIP]

This project is adaptable to the size and weight of your materials. The larger example pictured uses size 6° seed beads instead of size 8°s and 16-gauge wire instead of 18-gauge.

MATERIALS

20 size 8° seed beads

1 size 6° seed bead

1 large disc bead (40–60 mm) with a large hole

1 medium disc bead or rondelle (10–20 mm)

1 small disc bead (8–14 mm) with a large hole

1' (30.5 cm) of sterling silver 18-gauge half-hard wire

TOOLS

Flush cutters

Round-nose pliers

Crimping pliers

FINISHED SIZE

2" (5 cm)

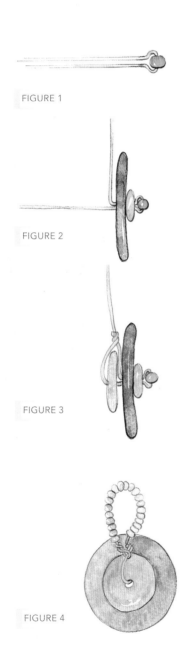

FIGURE 1

FIGURE 2

FIGURE 3

FIGURE 4

1 Use the wire to string the size 6° bead. Fold the wire around the bead, leaving a 4" (10 cm) tail and an 8" (20.5 cm) tail. Use the crimping pliers to fit the wire tightly to the bead. Bend the ends of the wire up together, making a sharp bend so the bead doesn't move **(Figure 1)**. Pull the wire tight with the pliers and make sharp angles when bending it.

2 Use both ends of wire to string the small disc and the large disc. Bend the 8" (20.5 cm) end of the wire sharply up behind the disc **(Figure 2)**.

3 Pass the short end of the wire through the remaining medium-size disc and bend it up sharply, backing the large disc with the medium-size disc. Wrap the short end of the wire around the long wire just above the medium-size disc. Coil 1–2 times and trim the end **(Figure 3)**.

4 String 20 size 8° seed beads on the long wire. Use your fingers to bend the wire into a loop. Wrap the end to the wire that backs the disc, coil 1–2 times, and trim **(Figure 4)**. Use crimping pliers to hide the tails.

The Evolution of a Starfish
Beadmaking Refined

This was the first starfish pendant I ever made, during my first summer living in Maine. My excitement at the temperate season on Maine's beaches was the inspiration for the form and colors. In Maine, we wait a long time for summer. We are excited when it's finally warm and it seems that the population celebrates by wearing summery colors.

As I've practiced lampworking and gained an understanding of how glass flows, I've become more skilled at creating the starfish I envisioned. Now I don't think much about the process and technical aspects of the bead-

CAROLYN RAMSAY

making while I make the starfish over the torch. It has become almost second nature to form the layers and accentuate the long, slender shape of the arms. I focus instead on combining opaque and transparent colors to make new shades; I try to give each little starfish a bit of its own personality.

I'm pleased that bead buyers respond to the shape as much as I do. The form is simple and elemental. Customers and I both like that they make great gifts, like giving someone a gold star—a star means, "You are super!" like a heart means "I love you."

Multistrand Necklace

The style of this necklace is a classic—many cultures and designers have their own versions. It highlights a large focal pendant, often a symbol or icon. I like multistrand necklaces with huge shells for centerpieces; in Africa and India many necklaces in this style feature large silver medallions.

[CHOOSING BEADS]

I like to use Czech seed beads or white hearts for the accent beads because, unlike tube-shaped Japanese seed beads, Czech beads are irregular in shape and have a rounded edge. This allows them to nestle into one another and drape well. The accent beads must support the pendant and shouldn't be visually stronger than the centerpiece. It's important that the pendant is large and heavy so it stays put in the center and creates visual symmetry.

[DESIGN TIP]

Making a multistrand necklace drape well is a challenge. This project uses my stringing trick to get all of the strands to look like they are resting comfortably on the wearer. By looping the ends to one another at the clasp, the strands rest more naturally.

MATERIALS

1 tube size 8° seed beads

Four 18" strands of 4mm (or smaller) beads

1 large pendant

Note: If the pendant's hole runs back-to-front, a wireworked bail may be necessary.

1 button with a shank

6 crimp tubes

5 beads to cover crimp tubes

10' (3 m) of .019 beading wire

TOOLS

Crimping pliers

Flush cutters

FINISHED SIZE

21" (53.5 cm)

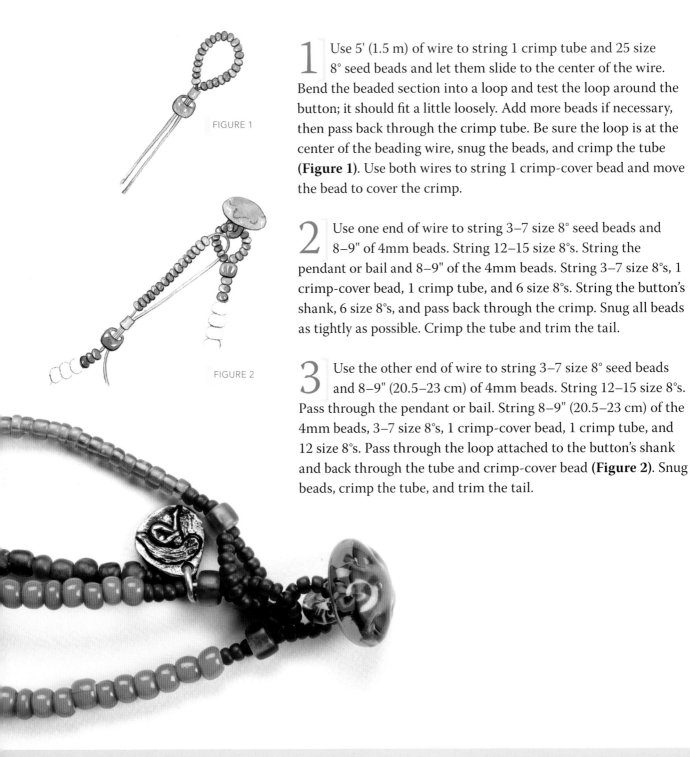

FIGURE 1

FIGURE 2

1 Use 5' (1.5 m) of wire to string 1 crimp tube and 25 size 8° seed beads and let them slide to the center of the wire. Bend the beaded section into a loop and test the loop around the button; it should fit a little loosely. Add more beads if necessary, then pass back through the crimp tube. Be sure the loop is at the center of the beading wire, snug the beads, and crimp the tube (**Figure 1**). Use both wires to string 1 crimp-cover bead and move the bead to cover the crimp.

2 Use one end of wire to string 3–7 size 8° seed beads and 8–9" of 4mm beads. String 12–15 size 8°s. String the pendant or bail and 8–9" of the 4mm beads. String 3–7 size 8°s, 1 crimp-cover bead, 1 crimp tube, and 6 size 8°s. String the button's shank, 6 size 8°s, and pass back through the crimp. Snug all beads as tightly as possible. Crimp the tube and trim the tail.

3 Use the other end of wire to string 3–7 size 8° seed beads and 8–9" (20.5–23 cm) of 4mm beads. String 12–15 size 8°s. Pass through the pendant or bail. String 8–9" (20.5–23 cm) of the 4mm beads, 3–7 size 8°s, 1 crimp-cover bead, 1 crimp tube, and 12 size 8°s. Pass through the loop attached to the button's shank and back through the tube and crimp-cover bead (**Figure 2**). Snug beads, crimp the tube, and trim the tail.

4 Use 5' (1.5 m) of wire to string 12 size 8° seed beads and let them slide to the center of the wire. Use one end of wire to pass through the loop formed in Step 1. Use both ends of wire to string 1 crimp tube. Snug the beads at the midpoint of the wire and crimp the tube. Use both wires to string 1 crimp-cover bead **(Figure 3)**.

5 Use one end of wire to string 3–7 size 8° seed beads and 8–9" (20.5–23 cm) of 4mm beads. String 12–15 size 8°s. Pass through the pendant or bail. String 8–9" (20.5–23 cm) of the 4mm beads, 3–7 size 8°s, 1 crimp-cover bead, 1 crimp tube, and 12 size 8°s. Pass through the loop formed in Step 3, back through the crimp tube. Snug the beads, crimp the tube, and trim the tail **(Figure 4)**.

6 Use the remaining wire to string 3–7 size 8° seed beads and 8–9" (20.5–23 cm) of 4mm beads. String 12–15 size 8°s. Pass through the pendant or bail. String 8–9" of the 4mm beads, 3–7 size 8°s, and 1 crimp tube. Pass through the crimp-cover bead and loop formed in Step 3. Pass back through the crimp-cover bead and crimp bead. Snug the beads, crimp the tube, and trim the tail **(Figure 5)**.

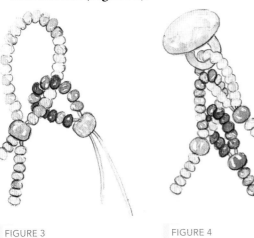

FIGURE 3

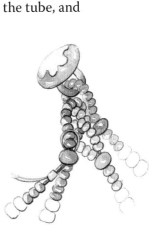

FIGURE 4

FIGURE 5

Berber-Style Hoop Earrings

The jewelry made by the nomadic Berber tribes of North Africa brings together a variety of textures. Glass, stone, silver, and fiber components work collectively to create a breathtaking aesthetic. This is a simple pair of earrings, but the contrast of the materials creates visual complexity.

[CHOOSING BEADS]

Choose small, lightweight beads for earrings. Vary the materials. To create a more earthy texture, try adding a semiprecious stone or shell for an accent bead. There are fewer than 15 beads in each of these earrings, but they take a long time to assemble because certain elements just don't seem to "sit right" while I'm making them. Make adjustments and be willing to start over, but also remember that they're supposed to look rough and weathered.

[DESIGN TIP]

If you like the look of this design but prefer wearing smaller earrings, use smaller hoops. The smaller pair shown on page 78 is made on 16 mm hoops (with .05 [1.3 mm]" diameter tube).

MATERIALS

9 pairs size 5° and 6° seed beads
5 pairs 6–9mm glass rondelles with large holes (greater than .09" [2.2 mm])
1 pair 8x10mm glass ovals
1 pair Thai silver discs with holes greater than .09"
1 pair silver accent beads
1 pair silver charms with large bails or jump rings
1 pair silver "endless" 22mm hoops with a .09" (2.3 mm) dia. tube
24" (61 cm) of 4-ply waxed linen in main color
8" (20.5 cm) of 4-ply waxed linen in second color

TOOLS

Scissors

FINISHED SIZE

1½" (3.8 cm) long

FIGURE 1

FIGURE 2

1 Cut the 24" (61 cm) piece of waxed linen into four 6" (15 cm) lengths and cut the 8" piece into two 4" (10 cm) pieces.

2 Fold the center of two 6" (15 cm) lengths of linen around 1 hoop at its center. Use 1 tail to tie a fringe knot around the other 3 tails, doubling and securing all of the ends (**Figure 1**). Use two strands to string 1 seed bead, 1 glass oval, and 1 seed bead. Tie an overhand knot to secure beads. Use 1 strand to string 1 seed bead, 1 rondelle, and 1 seed bead. Tie an overhand knot. Use the fourth strand to string 3 seed beads and tie an overhand knot. Cut tails to ¼" (6 mm).

3 String 1 charm onto the hoop. String rondelles and 1 silver disc onto the hoop, putting the larger beads at the center of the hoop and the smaller beads on the sides.

4 On the side that has the open end of the tube, tie a 4" (10 cm) piece of the second color of waxed linen in a fringe knot above the last bead. Use one strand to string 1 seed bead. Tie an overhand knot to secure the bead. Use the other strand to string 1 seed bead, 1 silver bead, and 1 seed bead. Tie an over-hand knot. Cut tails to ¼" (6 mm) (**Figure 2**).

A Signature Tag
Making Collectible Artwork

I teach my bead and jewelry techniques all over the world because I believe that sharing techniques and ideas helps me to evolve and expand the possibilities in the medium. But as a working artist, I also want my ideas to appeal to others, and I must sell my bead and jewelry art so that I can continue to make new work.

Years ago while watching *Antiques Roadshow,* I realized that I really wanted to make my art identifiable as my own. I wanted someone to be able to recognize my jewelry years later as mine, the way that the experts on the show can attribute a piece to a maker centuries later. Though the colors and techniques in my work are distinctive, not all buyers and collectors know about the range of beads and jewelers working today. I needed a way for potential owners of my work to recognize a piece as mine, the same way a signature on a painting traces it back to the artist. I spend time with customers at shows writing down the materials used in their pieces and telling them about unique attributes of their new purchases. My hand in making and choosing the materials is a distinguishable part of the design. The signature tag assures buyers that that the selection of the unique materials and quality of workmanship is my own.

As a crazy college student, before I started my little business, I had my upper arm tattooed with an angel inscribed with an "S" following the lines of her body. The angel's wings particularly appealed to me because I have dreams of flying. When I started my business and needed a logo my mom said, "Why don't you have that thing on your arm be your logo?" It was a brilliant idea.

I showed the design to Cynthia and Greg of Green Girl Studios. I have been drawn to Cynthia's ethereal designs for many years, and I had heard they did some custom work. I looked forward to seeing what they would create from the image and was delighted with the dimension they gave the angel. Now the pewter tag lays claim on my work. I now "sign" all of the pieces I make with the signature tag.

Fringey Bracelet

I like to wear several bracelets at once. (I'm a "more is more" girl.) This piece is made up of several strands clasped together, which gives it the look of many bracelets but the ease of one.

[CHOOSING BEADS]

* Think small! There are a lot of beads on this bracelet, so try to find small tubes and seed beads. Large beads will wear heavily on the waxed linen.
* Keep the color scheme and bead motifs simple. There's a lot of texture created by the knots and strings, so consider playing down other elements if you want to create a look that seems intentional and attractive.

[DESIGN TIP]

If your tube-shaped beads have large holes, like lampworked beads, you can double the strands of waxed linen or use seed beads at the ends to stop the knots from slipping into the holes, as on the red-and-black bracelet on page 82.

MATERIALS

About 40 size 8° seed beads
4 size 6° seed beads (A)
40–50 size 6° seed beads (B)
3 size 2° seed beads to use as crimp-cover beads
3 round 6–8 mm beads
30–36 glass 10–15mm cone- or tube-shaped beads
15–18 glass 6x4mm tubes
1 button with shank
1 silver accent bead
3 crimp tubes
2' (61 cm) of .024 beading wire
4–6 yd (3.7–5.5 m) of 4-ply waxed linen
20" (51 cm) of fiber (silk cord, textured yarn, etc.)

TOOLS

Crimping pliers
Flush cutters
Scissors

FINISHED SIZE

7¾" (19.5 cm)

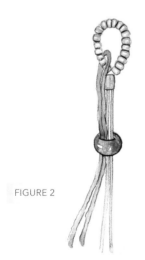

FIGURE 1

FIGURE 2

1 Use both ends of 4" (10 cm) of waxed linen to tie an over-hand knot leaving a very small loop. Use one end of linen to string one 10–15mm tube or cone bead. Tie an overhand knot to prevent the bead from slipping off. Trim the end, leaving a ¼" (6 mm) tail. Repeat with the other end of linen (**Figure 1**). Repeat entire step to make a total of sixteen units.

2 Use the beading wire to string 20 size 8° seed beads. Use both ends of wire to string 1 crimp tube. Center the seed beads on the wire and snug the crimp bead up to them so the loop is tight. Test the button to be sure it easily passes through the loop. Adjust the number of beads in the loop if necessary, then snug the beads, and crimp the tube.

3 Use the fiber to string the loop just formed. Center the fiber just above the crimp tube and fold the ends of fiber toward the ends of wire. Use both strands of fiber and both ends of wire to string 1 crimp-cover bead (**Figure 2**). (You may need to wax the ends of the fiber to get them through the bead.)

4 | Use one end of wire to string 2 size 8°s, about 5" of size 6°s (B), and 2 size 8°s. Use the other wire to string 3 size 8°s and one 6×4mm tube. String the loop of 1 tassel and one 6×4mm tube sixteen times. String 3 size 8°s. Snug the beads to make sure the two beaded strands are the same length **(Figure 3)**. Add size 8° seed beads to even the strands if necessary. Use both ends of wire to string 1 crimp tube. Snug the beads, crimp the tube, and trim one of the wire tails. Set aside.

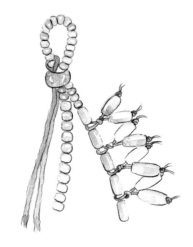

FIGURE 3

5 | Use both ends of fiber to tie an overhand knot ¾" (2 cm) from where it is attached to the loop of beads. Continue tying overhand knots every ¾" (2 cm) for a total of five knots. Use both ends of fiber and the wire tail to string 1 crimp-cover bead **(Figure 4)**. Snug the bead so that it covers the crimp tube. Make sure the fiber strand is the same length as the beaded strands, then use both ends of fiber to tie an overhand knot just after the crimp cover bead.

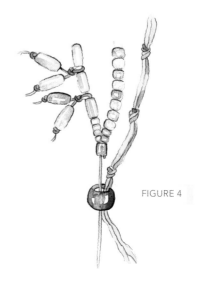

FIGURE 4

6 | Use the remaining wire tail to string 1 size 6° (A) and 1 round three times. String 1 size 6° (A), 1 crimp-cover bead, 1 crimp tube, and the silver accent bead. If the button has a thin metal shank, pass the beading wire through the shank and back through the crimp **(Figure 5)**, snug the beads, crimp the tube, and trim the wire. If the button has a larger shank, string 6 size 11° seed beads before and after adding the button.

FIGURE 5

Spiny Knotted Bracelet

When I invented this technique, I was just playing around with macramé knots. I noticed I could hang beads between each knot to create a lush texture. A New York customer called this bracelet "a party on your wrist." Now I think of these pieces as party bracelets—wearing one truly improves your mood.

[CHOOSING BEADS]

* When I make a knotted bracelet, I most often work in a theme or specific color palette. (It is fun to make a "kitchen sink" bracelet with every color and motif, but themed, thoughtful renditions are often the most timeless and beautiful.) I usually use 15 different types of beads in a bracelet, but they are all related in color, motif, or finish.
* The holes in the beads should be large enough to accommodate the waxed linen; the hole (or holes) in the button should be large enough to accommodate three or more pieces of waxed linen.

[DESIGN TIP]

All knots formed in the piece will be made with strands of pearl cotton and all the beads will be strung onto the waxed linen. Use more knots between beads if your beads are large or your bracelet seems crowded.

MATERIALS

50 assorted 3.5–10mm beads of various shapes, colors, and styles

40 Czech pressed-glass 10–15mm long daggers or other top-drilled beads

1 two-hole or shank button

7 yd (6.4 m) of 4-ply waxed linen

1 skein size 5 pearl cotton

TOOLS

Scissors and/or flush cutters

Flat-nose pliers

Size 20 tapestry needle

Homasote beading board

T-pins

FINISHED SIZE

7¼" (18.5 cm)

1 Cut six 1 yd (.9 m) pieces of waxed linen. Group the pieces together so that the ends match up. Find the midpoint of the group and use one of the pieces of linen to wrap around the other five, binding the strands together and coiling tightly **(Figure 1)**. Continue coiling until you've wrapped a length long enough to serve as your button's loop **(Figure 2)**. Pinch the group together at the beginning and end of the coil and use a second piece of linen from the group to wrap the remaining eleven ends of linen together **(Figure 3)**. Pin the loop to the board.

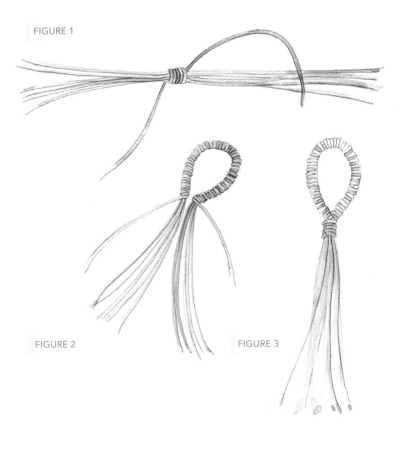

FIGURE 1

FIGURE 2

FIGURE 3

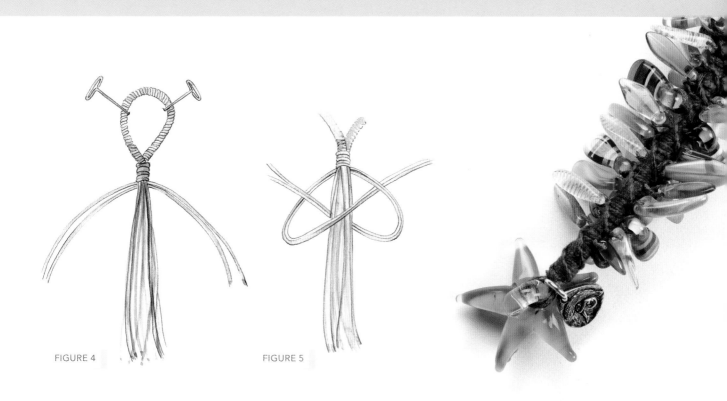

FIGURE 4

FIGURE 5

2 Cut two 4' (10 cm) pieces of pearl cotton. Place the pearl cotton strands behind the linen strands so that the midpoints of the pearl cotton strands sit just below the bottom coil formed in Step 1 **(Figure 4)**.

3 Place the pearl cotton strands on the left of the loop over the core of waxed linen strands in the shape of a "4." Wrap the pearl cotton strings from the right of the loop over the other pearl cotton strands, up and under the core strands, and out from the center of the "4" **(Figure 5)**. Carefully pull both sides tight and up into place so that the knot sits below the coils of waxed linen. (This first knot is tricky because there isn't a previous knot to hold the strings in place.) Repeat entire step two more times, making sure that each knot is snug enough to cover the waxed linen strands inside.

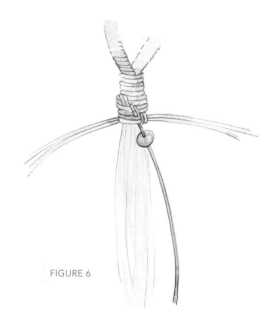

FIGURE 6

4 Pull one of the longer strands of waxed linen from the center of the group away from the others. Use this strand to string 1 small bead and push the bead up near the base of the knots (**Figure 6**). Replace the strand back in the group of core strings. Use the pearl cotton strands to form a knot as in Step 3, but before tightening it into place, pull the bead above the surface of the knotting. As you pull the pearl cotton strands tight, hold the bead out to "trap" it outside the knots. It should appear to be dangling off on a little loop (**Figure 7**). Give each bead some slack so that the bracelet has some movement but knot firmly and consistently to keep it flexible and strong. If the beads are heavy or have large holes, thread more than one strand of waxed linen through a bead; if a bead's hole is too small for the waxed linen to fit, divide a strand by unrolling it and pulling the 4 plies into two 2-ply pieces.

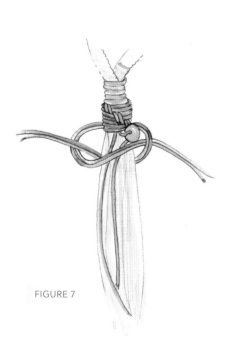

FIGURE 7

5 Repeat Step 4, adding 1 bead per knot and randomly using the sizes and shapes of beads, until you have about 3" of beads knotted to the bracelet. Use a different strand of waxed linen every time to keep the front and sides of the bracelet full. Keep checking on the back "spine" of the bracelet. It shouldn't include beads and should spiral around. If it doesn't, try making looser loops and shoving each knot up, under the bead, so there is no waxed linen showing through the stitches. To keep the knotting strings moving around the core, switch the left-hand strings over to the right and the right-hand strings under the waxed linen to the left (or clockwise) every six or seven knots **(Figure 8)**.

6 When pearl cotton strands get short, add new strands to one side at a time, replacing the shorter side first: Cut a 4' piece of pearl cotton. Place the old pearl cotton strands (the ones you're replacing) in the center with the waxed linen core strings. Loop the new strings around the center core group, meeting their ends on the side you're replacing **(Figure 9)**. Form a knot, as in Step 3, using the new strings to form the "4." After adding a few more beads and knots, repeat the step to add pearl cotton strands to the other side.

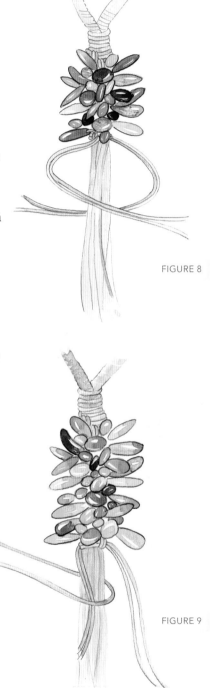

FIGURE 8

FIGURE 9

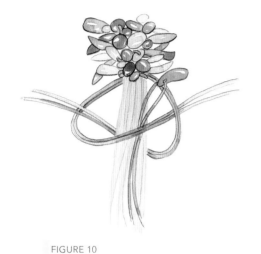

FIGURE 10

FIGURE 11

7 To add waxed linen (core strands), cut a 2' (61 cm) piece of waxed linen, string 1 bead, and fold the ends together with the bead at the linen's midpoint. Place it with the other core strings and knot over the new piece, binding it into the center with the other core strings (**Figure 10**).

8 Attach the button when you have knotted for about two-thirds of the bracelet length, or about 3" (7.5 cm). Use as many of the waxed linen strands as possible to string the button. Wrap the bracelet around your wrist and place the button on the waxed linen where it will comfortably fit. Hold the button in place on the waxed linen and fold the strands up toward the loop (**Figure 11**).

9 Continue knotting and adding beads as before, making sure to knot tightly over the folded-back core strings to secure them back into the bracelet and keep the button from slipping **(Figure 12)**. When you're about ¾" (2 cm) from reaching the button, stop adding beads and just make knots. While making the last seven to eight knots, clip the waxed linen strings from the core right at their base, being careful not to cut the ones that hold the button on. To keep the width of the core consistent, clip one core strand per knot and save cutting a few core strings for the last knot, especially those that were used for the last 3 or 4 beads. After all of the core strings have been clipped and your knots are close to the base of the button, use a square knot to tie the groups of pearl cotton together **(Figure 13)**.

10 Thread the pearl cotton tails on the tapestry needle and push the needle up inside the knotted core about 1" (2.5 cm) **(Figure 14)**. Use flat-nose pliers to pull the needle through the core. Trim all tails.

FIGURE 12

FIGURE 13

FIGURE 14

Flower Drop Earrings

This is another kinetic piece, like the Spinning Bead Pendant on page 68. Protrusions and moving pieces give a celebratory feeling to my designs. The flowers in these earrings spin like pinwheels, making the flower motif even more joyful.

[CHOOSING BEADS]

* Choose vibrant focal beads and neutral green accent beads to make a traditional pair like the ones at near left. The contrast of the neutral background highlights the vibrant shades of the petals, as it does on a real flower.
* You're not limited to flowers for these earrings; for a different look, choose a pair of lightweight discs with large holes for the focal beads.

[DESIGN TIP]

Pull tight on the wire when wrapping. To make the seed bead in front stay firmly in place, it helps to make sharp bends in the wire when the two ends are folded up together in the first step.

MATERIALS

10 size 8° seed beads
2 size 6° seed beads
2 glass 8mm discs
2 glass 8mm discs with large holes
2 glass 20mm flower beads or discs
2' (61 cm) of sterling silver 20-gauge half-hard wire
2 ear wires

TOOLS

Wire cutters
Crimping pliers
Round-nose pliers

FINISHED SIZE

2" (5 cm)

FIGURE 1

1 Use 12" (30 cm) of wire to string 1 size 6° seed bead on the wire, letting it settle at the wire's center. Fold both ends of the wire around the bead, using the crimping pliers to fit it tightly. Bend the ends of the wire up together, making sharp bends so the bead doesn't move (**Figure 1**).

2 Use both ends of wire to string 1 large-hole disc and the front side of the flower bead (**Figure 2**).

3 Use one end of the wire to make a sharp bend behind the flower. Use the other end of wire to string 1 disc, then make a sharp bend in the wire behind the disc in the same direction as the other wire (**Figure 3**).

FIGURE 2

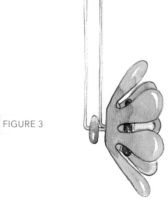

FIGURE 3

FIGURE 4

4 | Use the wire behind the disc to wrap one to two times around the wire behind the flower just above the disc, and trim the end of the coiled wire (**Figure 4**).

5 | Use the remaining wire to string 5 size 8° seed beads. Use round-nose pliers to make a wrapped loop with 2–3 coils so that the beads fit snugly on the wire. Trim the wire end and use crimping pliers to round out the sharp wire ends (**Figure 5**). Attach the ear wire to the wrapped loop.

6 | Repeat Steps 1–5 to make the second earring.

FIGURE 5

Berber-Style Necklace

As in the Berber-Style Hoop Earrings project on page 76, this necklace gets its marvelous texture by using different types of materials, all worked together. Grouping the strands together at certain focal points gives the necklace a rhythm, a pattern that unites the elements. I like the "random-on-purpose" look of ethnic jewelry and often try to create that feeling in my own designs.

[CHOOSING BEADS]

* Choose pendants with large bails to accommodate several strands.
* Keeping the seed beads close in color will allow you to use more varied focal elements. If the pendants are more similar, you can liberally vary the shades of seed beads.

[DESIGN TIP]

This necklace is adjustable because it ties in the back. If you prefer a necklace with a button or clasp, follow the finishing instructions for the Wispy Necklace on page 44 (basic clasp) or Multistrand Necklace with Pendant on page 72 (button-clasp).

MATERIALS

15 g size 8° seed beads (A)

10 g size 8° seed beads in each of two colors (B) and (C)

4 size 6° seed beads

5 pendants

30–40 sterling silver accent beads, at least 8 of which will fit over crimp tubes

2 silver 12mm soldered jump rings

8 crimp tubes

10' (25.5 cm) of 4-ply waxed linen

6' (1.8 m) of .019 beading wire

TOOLS

Scissors

Crimping pliers

Flush cutters

FINISHED SIZE

25" (63.5 cm)

1 Use 18" (45.5 cm) of beading wire to string 1 crimp tube and 1 soldered jump ring. Pass back through the tube and crimp. Repeat to attach a total of four 18" (45.5 cm) strands of wire to the same jump ring.

2 Use 1 strand of wire to string 1 crimp-cover bead. String about 2" (5 cm) of size 8°s (A), randomly placing 1 or 2 silver accent beads between size 8°s. String 1 pendant and about 2" (5 cm) of size 8°s (A) with silver accent beads five times, making sure the pendants are evenly spaced. String 1 crimp-cover bead, 1 crimp tube, and the other jump ring. Pass back through the tube and, keeping the tension looser than usual, crimp and trim the wire.

3 Repeat Step 2, using size 8°s (A) and passing through a pendant after every 2" of seed beads and silver accent beads.

FIGURE 1

4 Repeat Step 3, using size 8°s (B). Repeat Step 3 again, using size 8°s (C) **(Figure 1)**.

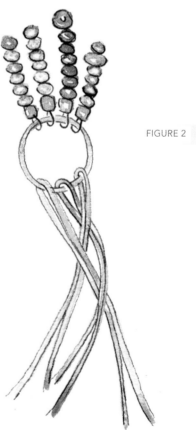

FIGURE 2

5 Use 20" (51 cm) of waxed linen to string 1 jump ring. Center the ring on the linen and press the two sides together so they stick slightly. Repeat for a total of three sets of linen. Braid the sets together for about 5" (12.5 cm) **(Figure 2)**. Divide the ends into two groups of three and use the two groups to form a square knot. Use your fingers to roll the ends of one group together and string 1 size 6° seed bead. Tie an overhand knot to secure the seed bead and trim the tails to ⅓" (8 mm).

6 Repeat Step 5 for the second jump ring.

Fiber Bangle

I was very excited to find the emBead cord—another bead-friendly fibrous material! It is shiny and soft, like stuffed, puffy baby mobiles. It is comfortable and silky to touch. The texture and structure of the material inspired me to use it not only for traditional stringing (passing it through the beads) but also to sew beads onto it. The sewn beads trap the strung beads so they can't move around.

[CHOOSING BEADS]

* If you are a lampworker (or are lucky enough to know a lampworker who will make you beads for this project), it may be helpful to know that the big-hole beads shown here were made on a ⅜" (1 cm) mandrel.
* Large or heavy beads are okay for the strung beads, but avoid them for the sewn beads because the thread used for sewing can't bear much weight.

[DESIGN TIP]

The sizing of the bracelet is important—make it just large enough to fit over your hand. If it's too large, the weighty front of the bracelet will turn around to the back. The unbeaded inside of the bracelet stays comfortably on your arm.

MATERIALS

2 size 8° or 6° seed beads

2 glass 6mm rondelles

2 disc-shaped beads (½–¾" diameter)

3 donuts or rondelles with 1cm holes

Size D Nymo beading thread

9" (23 cm) of emBead cord (⅜" gauge)

9" (23 cm) of sterling silver 20-gauge soft wire

TOOLS

Scissors

Round-nose pliers

Flush cutters

Size 10 sharp beading needle

FINISHED SIZE

7¾" (19.5) circumference

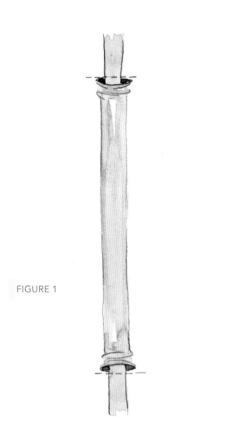

FIGURE 1

1 Pull back the ends of cord to reveal the inner core and cut ¾" (2 cm) off each end **(Figure 1)**. Pull the fabric back over the ends so the core is recessed into the ends. Fit the end of the wire into the sleeve and down the side so that the wire slips easily down through the entire length of the cord. Bend the wire/cord around your wrist to make an oval, making sure the seam of the cord is on the inside of the bangle.

2 Use the wire/cord to string the donuts/rondelles. Use round-nose pliers to form simple loops at both ends of the wire. Open one simple loop, attach it to the other simple loop, and close the loop so that the wire is permanently linked **(Figure 2)**.

FIGURE 2

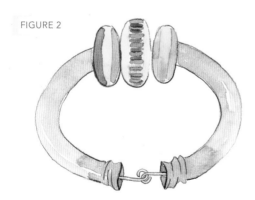

3 Tuck the raw edges of the cord inside to form a clean edge for hemming. Use the needle to string a comfortable length of thread. Center the needle on the thread and use an overhand knot to tie the ends together. Use whipstitch to sew the edges of the cord together, starting and ending at its seam **(Figure 3)**. Slide the donuts/rondelles around the bangle to cover the stitching and push them close together.

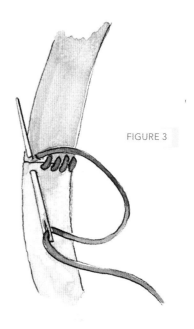

FIGURE 3

4 With the needle and thread, sew on the discs outside the donuts/rondelles to hold them in place: Rethread the needle with double thread (as in Step 2). Pass up through the cord at its seam. String 1 disc, one 6mm rondelle, and 1 seed bead. Pass back through the rondelle, disc, and cord, keeping the thread tension loose enough to avoid compressing the cord. Sew through all the components several times to secure. Knot the thread securely at the seam and trim. Repeat entire step on the other side of the donuts/rondelles, trapping them in place **(Figure 4)**.

5 If necessary, reform the bracelet into an oval so that will fit over your hand.

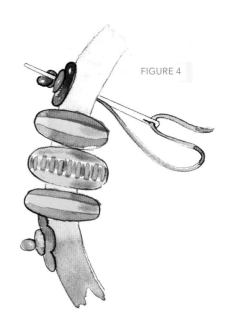

FIGURE 4

Pearly Sewn Collar

A favorite teacher once told me that a piece of jewelry should look good from ten feet away, two feet away, and should offer something new and more beautiful when examined up close. Though this may be the most time-consuming piece in the book, I feel that the delicate beauty it offers when examined closely is worth every second of work. I also love how the collar sounds. If you shake it, it tinkles softly.

[CHOOSING BEADS]

* The lush texture of this necklace stays organized because of the pattern made by the disc beads on the band. Use a bold shape or color for those focal elements; they give rhythm to the design. The beads can be plain and free of motif because the alternating patterns create interest.

* Choose thin-walled and lightweight beads. Nymo and silk aren't suited to heavy beads or rough perforations. If necessary, use a reamer to grind away rough spots around the holes.

[DESIGN TIP]

When sewing beads on, keep the thread taut but not pulled too forcefully. You don't want the beads to be sewn on so tightly that the integrity of the thread is compromised. If you have to use large or heavy beads, sew through them many times.

MATERIALS

12 size 8° seed beads
24 Czech pressed-glass 6x9mm teardrops
12 thin lightweight glass discs, each 10–14mm
About sixty 3mm pearls
About 90 lightweight 6–8mm shells
Twelve 6mm sequins
30" (76 cm) of 1" (25 cm) hem tape
30" (76 cm) of 1" (25 cm) satin ribbon
1 large sheet Lacy's Stiff Stuff
All-purpose sewing thread
Size D Nymo beading thread
Size F silk thread

TOOLS

Scissors
Size 10 sharp beading needles
All-purpose sewing needles
Straight pins

FINISHED SIZE

21" (53.5 cm)

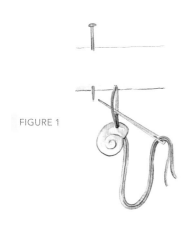

FIGURE 1

1 Use two straight pins to mark the hem tape at 10" (25.5 cm) increments. Use a sewing needle to thread the silk. Slide the needle to the middle of the silk and use both ends of silk to tie an overhand knot. Beginning at the first straight pin, sew on teardrops and shells to the middle section of the hem tape near the bottom edge: Pass the needle through the hem tape at one edge of the first mark, string 1 shell, and hold the shell ¾" (2 cm) from the hem tape. Weave the needle between the two strands of thread three or four times back and forth up toward the hem tape to give the silk a twisted appearance **(Figure 1)**, then pass back through the hem tape.

2 Continue adding dangling shells and teardrops at ¼" increments **(Figure 2)**. For a fuller collar, add a second layer of shells and teardrops ¼" (6mm) above the first layer. Complete the middle 10" (25.5 cm) of the hem tape in this manner.

FIGURE 2

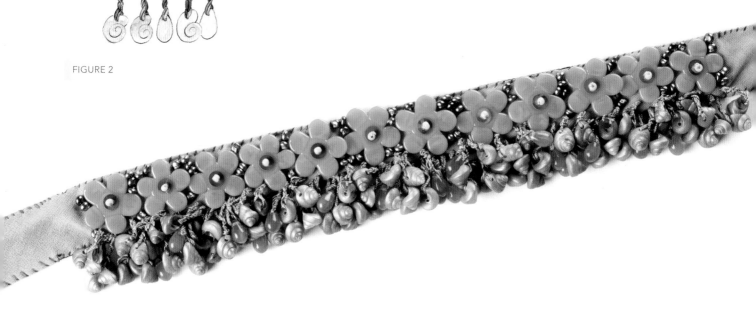

3 Use scissors to cut a 10½ × ⅞" (26.5 × 2.2 cm) strip of Lacy's Stiff Stuff. Pin the strip to the back of the hem tape, covering the stitches made in Step 2. Thread the size 10 sharp needle with Nymo thread. Slide the needle to the middle of the thread and use both ends of thread to tie an overhand knot (**Figure 3**). At the center of the piece, sew through the Stiff Stuff and hem tape, string 1 disc bead, 1 sequin, and 1 size 8° seed bead. Pass back through the sequin, disc, and fiber base (**Figure 4**). Tie an overhand knot and seat it snugly on the back of the Stiff Stuff. Repeat the stitch again, passing through the same beads to give the piece more strength. Repeat to attach all of the discs in this manner, leaving about ⅛" (3 mm) between the discs.

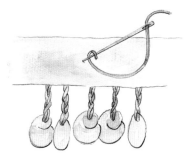

FIGURE 3

4 Use Nymo to sew on the pearls randomly, filling in the spaces between the discs: Stitch through the back of the piece, string 1 pearl and pass back through the hem tape and Lacy's Stiff Stuff.

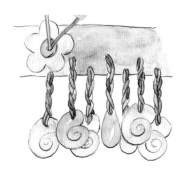

FIGURE 4

5 To back the hem tape, remove all pins, line up the ribbon and hem tape, and pin the ends together. Trim the ribbon and hem tape to fit, cutting the ends at an angle, leaving long enough ends to tie in a square knot at the back of the neck, about 6" (15 cm) on each side of the beaded section. Using the sewing thread and starting at the center of the piece, whipstitch the ribbon to the hem tape on the edges. When you reach the ends of the collar, tuck the raw edges of hem tape and ribbon inside before stitching to give the ends a clean finish.

Spiny Knotted Necklace

The look of the Spiny Knotted Necklace reminds me of the bottom of the ocean. My first few Spiny Knotted necklaces were ocean-themed in blues and greens, with sea shells interspersed. I suggest making at least one Spiny Knotted Bracelet (see page 84) before attempting the necklace. The two bead-encrusted tendrils come to meet in the center and form a wild centerpiece that passes through a central channel. This neck-piece is surprisingly comfortable to wear because it's balanced and symmetrical, following the lines of the upper torso.

[CHOOSING BEADS]

* The hole or holes in the button should be large enough to accommodate twelve pieces of waxed linen.
* If you plan to dangle several pendants from the center, as I have in the necklace shown here, choose a large center bead with a hole at least ¾" (2 cm) in diameter. The ideal bead has an oval or double-barrel-shaped hole.

[DESIGN TIPS]

* It's fun to use more than one color of waxed linen!
* Think about scale when placing the beads for both the knotted section and the center. If the beads used in the knotted part are huge and the pendants hung from the center are small, the piece will be visually and physically uncomfortable.

MATERIALS

About 15 size 6° seed beads
300 assorted 3.5–10mm beads of various shapes, colors, and styles
200 Czech pressed-glass 10–15mm long daggers or other end-drilled beads
1 large 2-hole or shank button
1 large-hole focal bead
5–7 large drops and dangles for the centerpiece
40–50 yd (37–46 m) of 4-ply waxed linen
2 skeins of size 5 pearl cotton

TOOLS

Scissors and/or flush cutters
Flat-nose pliers
Size 20 tapestry needle
Homasote beading board
T-pins

FINISHED SIZE

21½" (54.5 cm) necklace length, with 4" (10 cm) long centerpiece

1 Cut twelve 5' (1.5 m) pieces of waxed linen. Group the pieces together so that the ends match up. Find the midpoint of the group and use one of the pieces of linen to wrap around the other eleven, binding the strands together and coiling tightly (**Figure 1**). Continue coiling until you've wrapped a length long enough to serve as your button's loop (**Figure 2**). Pinch the group together at the beginning and end of the coil and use a second piece of linen from the group to wrap the twenty-three remaining ends of linen together (**Figure 3**). Pin the loop to the board.

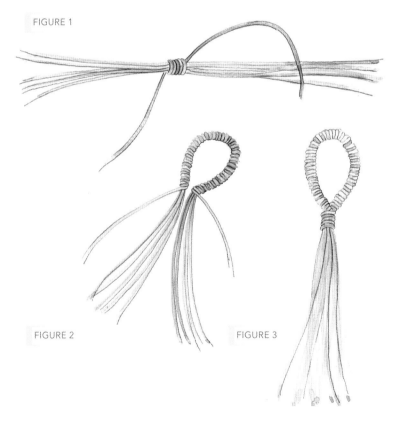

FIGURE 1

FIGURE 2

FIGURE 3

2 Cut two 6' (1.8 m) pieces of pearl cotton. Place the pearl cotton strands behind the linen strands so that the midpoints of the strands sit just below the bottom coil formed in Step 1 (**Figure 4**).

3 Wrap the pearl cotton strands on the left over the core of waxed linen strands in the shape of a "4." (Note that all the knots will be made with pearl cotton strands.) Wrap the pearl cotton strings from the right of the loop over the other pearl cotton strands, up and under the core strands, and out from the center of the "4" (**Figure 5**). Carefully pull both sides tight and up into place so that the knot sits below the coils of waxed linen. (This first knot is tricky, because there isn't a previous knot to hold the strings in place.)

4 Repeat Step 3 to make 3" (7.5 cm) of knots. To keep the knotting strings moving around the core, switch the left-hand strings over to the right and the right-hand strings under the waxed linen to the left (or clockwise) every six or seven knots.

FIGURE 4

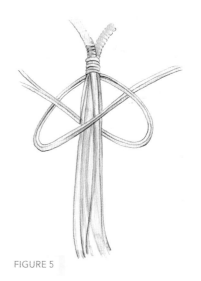

FIGURE 5

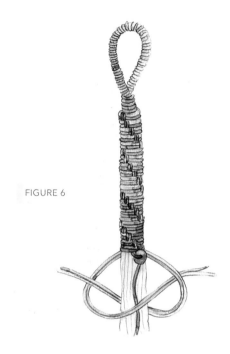

FIGURE 6

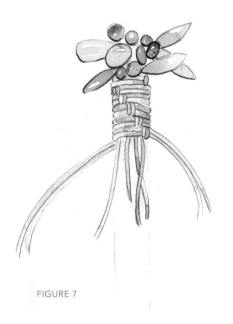

FIGURE 7

5 After 3" (7.5 cm) of knots have been placed, start adding beads. (*Note:* All the beads will be strung onto the waxed linen.) Pull one of the longer strands of waxed linen from the top and center of the group away from the others. String 1 small bead onto the strand of waxed linen and push it up near the base of the knots **(Figure 6)**. Replace the strand in the group of core strings. Use the pearl cotton to form a knot as in Step 3, but before tightening it into place, pull the bead above the surface of the knotting. As you pull the strands tight, hold the bead out to "trap" it outside the knots. It should appear to be dangling off on a little loop.

6 Repeat Step 5, adding 1 bead per knot and randomly using the sizes and shapes of beads, until you have about 7½" (19 cm) of beads knotted to the necklace. Use a different strand of waxed linen every time to keep the front and sides of the necklace full. Keep checking on the back "spine" of the necklace. It shouldn't include beads and should spiral around. If it doesn't try making looser loops and shoving each knot up, under the bead, so there is no waxed linen showing through the stitches. To add more waxed linen or pearl cotton, follow the directions in the Spiny Knotted Bracelet on pages 89–90. As you finish every 2" of knotting, insert a T-pin through the cord to hold your project firmly to the board.

7 When you've added beads to ¾" (2 cm) from the desired midpoint of the necklace, stop adding beads and just make knots. While making the last seven to eight knots, clip any short waxed linen and pearl cotton strands from the core right at their base **(Figure 7)**. To keep the width of the core consistent, clip one core strand per knot, leaving the long strands intact.

8 | Thread the remaining (long) pearl cotton strands on the tapestry needle and push the needle up inside the knotted core about 1" (2.5 cm) **(Figure 8)**. Use flat-nose pliers to pull the needle through the core. Trim the pearl cotton tails. Set aside.

9 | Cut twelve 5' (1.5 m) pieces of waxed linen to begin the other side. Repeat Step 1, but only coil at the midpoint of the strands for about 1" (2.5 cm). Roll the ends of the waxed linen together and string the button, moving it to the middle of the coiled section **(Figure 9)**, and continue as in Step 1.

10 | Repeat Steps 2–8 to make the second half of the necklace to match the first.

11 | Gather together the remaining waxed linen strands from both sides of the necklace and roll them together. Use the roll of strands to string the large-hole focal bead. Separate the strands into as many groups as you have charms, using four to six strands per charm, keeping in mind that the groups of strands need to fit through the bails and holes of the beads you've chosen to use as charms.

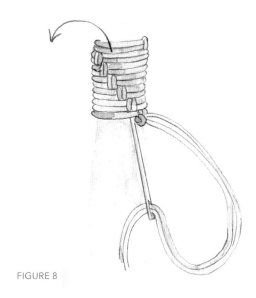

FIGURE 8

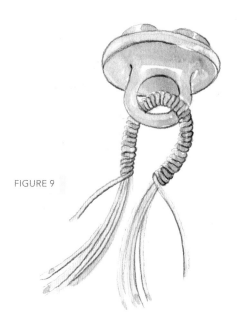

FIGURE 9

12 Charms can be attached in two different ways. When attaching charms, adjust the lengths of the dangling portion to create a full and textured centerpiece. It may be helpful to place one or two of the charms directly under the focal bead to keep the focal bead in place. To attach charms with small holes, pinch and roll the group of strands together and string 1 drop or dangle, leaving enough slack so that the piece hangs freely. Fold the strands back up toward the large-hole bead. Coil one strand around the others in the group, binding both sides together, and fasten with a buttonhole knot **(Figure 10)**. Coil this strand back up over the other strands, trimming the short pieces. When the coils have reached the large bead again, tie the wrapping strand to several of the inner strings with a buttonhole knot **(Figure 11)**. Add 1 seed bead or 1 Czech 4–6mm rondelle and tie a simple overhand knot to finish each end **(Figure 12)**. Trim all tails to ¼". Repeat entire step with the small-hole charms.

FIGURE 10

FIGURE 11

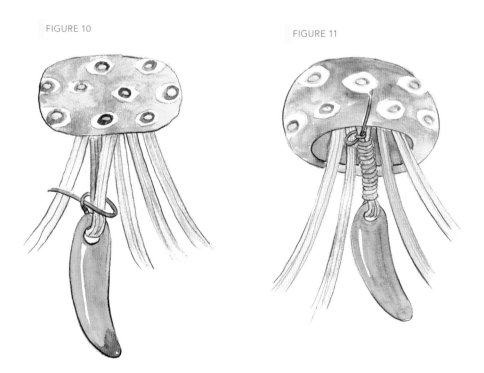

13 To attach charms with large holes, use one strand from the group to coil around the others. Coil down from the focal bead to the length that you want the charm to hang. Pass all strands through the charm. Use one strand to coil around the others for about ½–¾". Loop the strands around and use one strand to coil around all of the others, back up until you reach the focal bead. Separate the strands into two even groups and use both groups to tie a square knot to secure. Use 2–3 strands to string 1 seed bead. Tie an overhand knot and trim tails to ¼". Repeat with the other group of tails. Repeat entire step with any large-hole charms.

FIGURE 12

Button Brooch

This brooch features a single fancy button. Celebrate the beauty of this special piece by framing it with beads and knots. Outlining the round button with a frame of knots and repeating patterns of beads creates a well-balanced, radial shape. It reminds me of the icons I see in South America, where the frame becomes part of the art.

[CHOOSING BEADS]

The hole in the large donut must accommodate the shank of the button plus several strands of waxed linen. African donuts made of wound glass or resin have large holes and are perfect for this project. I have also used large, flat ceramic discs from Greece.

[DESIGN TIP]

For the sample with the heart button, I used bigger beads and doubled the strands of waxed linen to support their weight.

MATERIALS

20–35 glass 4–6mm rondelles
15–20 glass 8–12mm rondelles with large holes
1 large donut, 3–5cm in diameter with a very large hole
1 button with shank, 2cm in diameter
Pin pad and post
Pin back
1" (2.5 cm) circle of leather
2–3 yds (1.8–2.7 m) of 4-ply waxed linen
2-part jeweler's epoxy
Toothpicks
Cotton swab

TOOLS

Scissors

FINISHED SIZE

2¼" (5.5 cm)

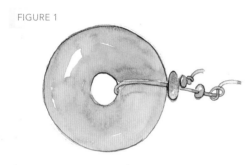

FIGURE 1

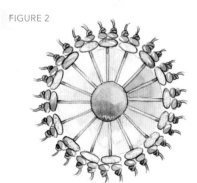

FIGURE 2

FIGURE 3

1 Use the ends of one or two 4" (10 cm) pieces of waxed linen to tie an overhand knot, leaving a ¼" (6 mm) tail. String one 4–6mm rondelle, one 8–12mm rondelle, and the donut. Pass back through the 8–12mm rondelle. Adjust the beads to sit on the edge of the donut. String one 4–6mm rondelle, snug the beads, and tie an overhand knot on top of the 4–6mm rondelle **(Figure 1)**. Trim the end, leaving a ¼" (6 mm) tail. Repeat entire step until the outside edge of the donut is full.

2 Use a cotton swab to remove any wax that may have transferred to the donut. Mix the epoxy according to package instructions and use a toothpick to spread the glue on the back of the button. Attach the button to one side of the donut **(Figure 2)**. Allow to dry.

3 Push the pin through the center of the piece of leather **(Figure 3)**. Mix more epoxy and generously apply it to the back of the leather and pin pad. Attach the leather to the other side of the donut. Allow to dry before putting on the pin back.

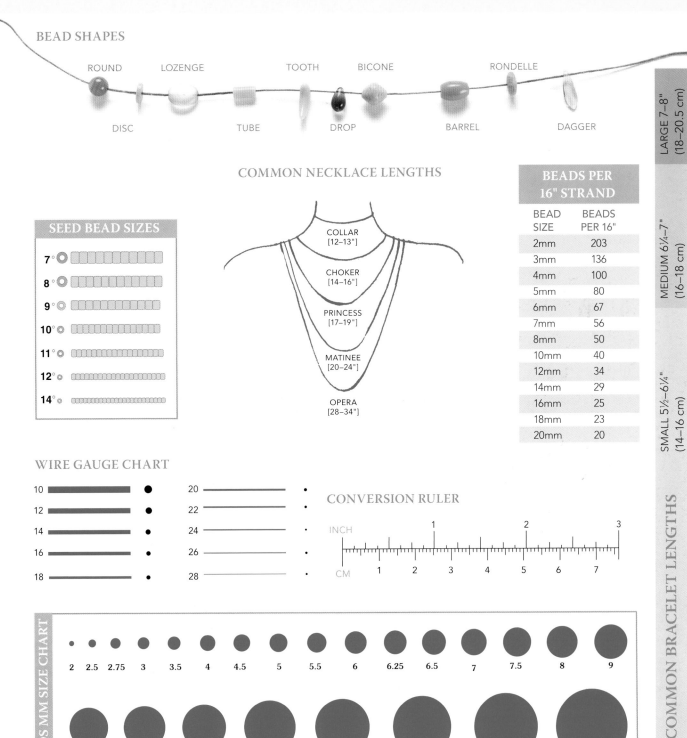

BEAD SHAPES

ROUND   LOZENGE   TOOTH   BICONE   RONDELLE

DISC   TUBE   DROP   BARREL   DAGGER

COMMON NECKLACE LENGTHS

COLLAR [12–13"]

CHOKER [14–16"]

PRINCESS [17–19"]

MATINEE [20–24"]

OPERA [28–34"]

SEED BEAD SIZES

7°
8°
9°
10°
11°
12°
14°

BEADS PER 16" STRAND

BEAD SIZE	BEADS PER 16"
2mm	203
3mm	136
4mm	100
5mm	80
6mm	67
7mm	56
8mm	50
10mm	40
12mm	34
14mm	29
16mm	25
18mm	23
20mm	20

WIRE GAUGE CHART

10
12
14
16
18

20
22
24
26
28

CONVERSION RULER

INCH   1   2   3

CM   1   2   3   4   5   6   7

ROUNDS MM SIZE CHART

2   2.5   2.75   3   3.5   4   4.5   5   5.5   6   6.25   6.5   7   7.5   8   9

10   11   12   14   15   16   18   20

LARGE 7–8" (18–20.5 cm)

MEDIUM 6¼–7" (16–18 cm)

SMALL 5½–6¼" (14–16 cm)

COMMON BRACELET LENGTHS

Materials and Supplies

All of the items below can be bought from the stores listed in Sources (see page 126).

STRING AND THREAD

] **NYMO** [is a popular nylon beading thread for small, lightweight beads. It comes in several colors and weights; the most common weights are B and D. D is the heaviest and most durable, and for that reason it is recommended for the projects in this book.

] **PEARL COTTON** [is a soft, versatile string that is not strong enough for stringing heavy beads, but it's a great fiber for knotting over other cords, knitting, or crocheting. It is sold in over a hundred colors and at least four weights.

] **SILK THREAD** [is ideal for knotting between beads. I also like to use silk when the thread will show in the final design because it has a beautiful sheen. It is available in over twenty colors and ten weights.

] **WAXED LINEN** [is strong natural fiber with a slightly sticky coating that works perfectly for coiling and knotting techniques. The best quality waxed linen is from Belfast, Ireland—it comes in over thirty colors and several plies. I like 4 ply for a good medium-weight fiber.

WIRE

] **BEADING WIRE** [is made from steel strands coated with nylon. It is extremely flexible and durable and comes in three weights. I use the heaviest weight, .024, for large beads. There are several brands of beading wire, but I find Soft Flex the strongest and most flexible.

] **STERLING SILVER WIRE** [is the most common and easily worked wire. The most common gauges are 18, 20, and 22, with the lower numbers designating thicker wire. Wire can be hard, half hard, or dead soft, depending on the degree of flexibility. (Wire can also be beautiful in gold and other metals.)

TOOLS

] **BEADING NEEDLES** [come in many types and varieties. I prefer short, sharp needles because I do more appliqué work than stringing. Pony brand needles are my favorite.

] **CRIMPING PLIERS** [are a special tool that folds and flattens a crimp bead so that it securely attaches two strands of beading wire; see Techniques (page 124) for instructions.

] **FLUSH CUTTERS** [are pliers designed especially for cutting wire in tight spots.

] **JEWELER'S FILES** [are used to smooth any rough spots in cut wire.

] **ROUND-NOSE PLIERS** [have two round tips, making them perfect for bending wire and forming loops.

] **T-PINS AND STRAIGHT PINS** [are both used for anchoring beading projects. T-pins are useful for stabilizing knotting projects against a Homasote bead board. Straight pins can be inserted through layers of fabric to temporarily bind them while stitching.

] **BEAD BOARDS** [are used to design and position beads while making jewelry. The kind I like is made from upholstered Homasote (a hardy compressed paperboard) that can be used for beadwork or display purposes. A pin can be firmly inserted many times and no mark is left in the board. They're easy to make—Homasote is available at home-building supply stores, and they can cut it up to your speci-fied dimensions. Cover the Homasote with durable fabric and staple the fabric to the back of the board. (My dad's upholstery shop makes batches of these for me.)

FINDINGS

] CRIMP BEADS [are tiny metal tube-shaped beads used to secure two or more strands of beading wire. To work effectively, they must be used with crimping pliers; see Techniques (page 124) for instructions.

] EAR WIRES [are simple findings for making drop or dangly earrings. Many styles are available, including hoops, French wires, and leverbacks.

] HEAD PINS [are pin-shaped findings that can be used to attach suspended beads to an ear wire, jump ring, or other finding.

] JUMP RINGS [hold jewelry components together. One can tie items to them or open and secure them to connect other pieces. They are sold open or soldered and are round or oval.

] PIN PADS, POSTS, AND BACKS [are simple findings for making brooches. The pad is glued or soldered to the piece, the post goes through the wearer's garment, and the pin back is used to secure the piece.

ADHESIVES

] JEWELER'S EPOXY [is a quick-setting and firm adhesive. Vigor 2-Part Jeweler's Epoxy is especially good for gluing glass, ceramic, plastic, metal, and wood. Setting time is just a few minutes. Directions are provided on the package.

] LACY'S STIFF STUFF [is a beading foundation for cabochon beading and bead appliqué. I like it for the structure it provides behind limp fabrics. It is very easy to sew through and stays stiff over time.

OTHER MATERIALS

] **FAIRY RIBBON** [is washed silk ribbon that is sold in 38" long pieces. It has a crinkly and rough but beautiful texture.

] **BIAS TAPE** [is a thin and porous foundation for sewing beads to a band. It must be used with lightweight beads and be backed by a ribbon or fabric. It is typically 1" in width. (This is the same hem tape used for lining the hem of a garment.) It can be found in a general craft or sewing store.

] **EMBEAD CORD** [is a soft cord or "welting" developed specifically for beading. Beads can be sewn to it or strung on it. It is available in a variety of colors and diameters.

] **LEATHER AND LEATHER CORDS** [are very durable and supple materials. Because it is difficult to sew through, leather is most easily used as a backing or cording. It is available in countless thicknesses and can be dyed in many colors.

] **SHELLS** [work great in beading projects to add a different texture or shape. It's convenient to find them with holes already in them. (If you want to drill holes, use a Dremel tool with a diamond bit. It is advisable to wear ear, eye, and lung protection.) All perforations should be reamed so that the hard shell doesn't wear through the string.

Basic Techniques

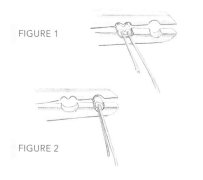

FIGURE 1

FIGURE 2

CRIMPING

String a crimp bead on the beading wire, then string the clasp or connector. Pass back through the crimp bead. Snug all the beads tight by pulling on the tail and redistributing any slack in the loop. Use the back teeth in the crimping pliers to make a U that separates the crimp tube into two channels that hold each wire separately **(Figure 1)**. Use the front teeth in the pliers to fold the channels together and squeeze tightly **(Figure 2)**. Clip the tail.

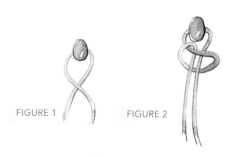

FIGURE 1   FIGURE 2

KNOTS

] FRINGE KNOT [

Hold the bead and cross the strands' tails **(Figure 1)**. Place the left strand around the other strand to form a loop behind both tails. Pass the tail through the loop from top to bottom **(Figure 2)**.

] OVERHAND KNOT [

Make a loop with the strand of thread. Tuck the back tail in front and pass it through the loop, pulling tightly.

] SQUARE KNOT [

Make an overhand knot, folding the right strand over the left. Make another overhand knot, but this time fold the left strand over the right before passing through the loop. Pull tightly.

WIREWORKING

] JUMP RINGS [

Jump rings connect wirework to findings. When you open or close a jump ring, use two pliers and bend the ends laterally, not apart. Add the finding and close the jump ring with the two pliers. Be sure to close the jump ring completely so the finding doesn't slip out. Do so by closing the ends slightly farther than where the ends match up—the wire will spring back to the right position.

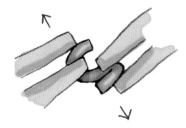

] WRAPPED BAIL [

Wrapped bails turn top-drilled beads, usually teardrops, into pendants. Center the bead on a 6" (15 cm) piece of wire. Bend both ends of the wire up the sides and across the top of the bead. Bend one end straight up at the center of the bead and wrap the other wire around it to form a few coils. Form a wrapped loop with the straight-up wire, wrapping it back down over the already formed coils. Trim the excess wire.

] WRAPPED LOOP [

Use pliers to bend the wire at a 90-degree angle ¼" (6 mm) above the top bead. Pull the end of the wire around the tip of the pliers and lay the tail across the bend. Insert the pliers into the loop again and pull the tail around the wire. Wrap the tail two to three times. Clip the tail.

Sources

[Glass Beads]

THE BEAD GOES ON...
Java glass beads, hill tribe silver, clasps, and more
14 Church Street
Vineyard Haven
Martha's Vineyard, MA 02568
(866) 861-2323
beadgoeson.com

THE BEADIN' PATH
Artist lampwork, Lucite, glass, and ethnic beads; vintage components; waxed linen; unique fibers; and beading foundations
15 Main Street
Freeport, ME 04032
(877) 92-BEADS (922-3237)
(207) 865-4785
beadinpath.com

GLASS GARDEN BEADS
Vintage beads and unique components
Northfield, Minnesota
(507) 645.0301
glassgardenbeads.com

THE MYKONOS
Greek ceramic beads, eye beads, leather cord, and unique components
(508) 778-0698
mykonosbeads.com

OSIRIS BEADS
Accent beads, including Czech seed beads and charlottes
Sue Oseland
(231) 933-4853
osirisbeads.com

RAVEN'S JOURNEY INC.
Czech glass beads and designer buttons
(206) 406-7491
theravenstore.com

TIKA
Ethnic beads, ancient beads, and imported components
Julie Joynt
(800) 459-3669
www.tikaimports.com

[Bead Artists]

All lampworked art beads shown in the projects as well as the bars in the Trapeze Necklace are by Stephanie Sersich Inc. See below for ordering information.

HAROLD COONEY
Manchester, New Hampshire

GAIL CROSMAN-MOORE
North Orange, Massachusetts
gailcrosmanmoore.com

KATE FOWLE MELENEY
katefowle.com

HERON GLASS
Mary Mullaney and Ralph Mossman
heronglass.com

MICHELE GOLDSTEIN
Salem, Oregon
michelegoldstein.com

SAGE AND TOM HOLLAND
Fox, Arkansas
(870) 363-4890
sageandtom@hotmail.com

AMY JOHNSON
Toronto, Ontario, Canada
ehmeglass.com

ANNE LENOX
Newton, Massachusetts
(617) 969-0866

KRISTINA LOGAN
Portsmouth, New Hampshire
kristinalogan.com

LINDA PERRIN
Ellsworth, Maine
atlanticartglass.com

ISIS RAY
Carnation, Washington
isisbeads@centurytel.net

STEPHANIE SERSICH
Portland, Maine
sssbeads.com

DUSTIN TABOR
Fayetteville, Arkansas
dustintabor.com

HEATHER TRIMLETT
heathertrimlett.com

[Findings + Materials]

EMBEAD
Soft, colorful embellishable cording for jewelry design
Susan Wohlgenant
embead.com

GREEN GIRL STUDIOS
Pewter and silver clasps, charms, and pendants
PO Box 19389
Asheville, NC 28815
greengirlstudios.com
(828) 298-2263

METALLIFEROUS
Wire, metal parts, and findings
metalliferous.com

SILK PAINTING IS FUN!
Silk cords, ribbons, and fibers
Ute Bernsen
(928) 607-2765
silkpaintingisfun.com

SOFT FLEX
Flexible beading wire and high-quality tools
(866) 925-3539
softflexcompany.com

Bibliography

Index

Dubin, Lois Sherr. *The History of Beads: From 30,000 BC to the Present.* New York: Harry N. Abrams, 1987.

Dunham, Bandhu Scott. *Contemporary Lampworking: A Practical Guide to Shaping Glass in the Flame.* Prescott, Arizona: Salusa Glassworks, 1997.

Francis, Peter, Jr. *Beads of the World: A Collector's Guide With Revised Price Reference.* Atglen, Pennsylvania: Schiffer Publishing, 1994.

Jenkins, Cindy. *Making Glass Beads.* Asheville, North Carolina: Lark Books, 1997.

Lankton, James W. *A Bead Timeline, Vol I: Prehistory to 1200 CE.* Washington, DC: The Bead Museum and The Bead Society of Greater Washington, 2003.

Liu, Robert K. *A Universal Aesthetic: Collectible Beads.* San Marcos, California: Ornament, 1995.

McCreight, Tim. *Design Language: Interpretive Edition.* Portland, Maine: Brynmorgen Press, 2006.

The following magazines may also be helpful:
Beadwork
Jewelry Artist
Stringing

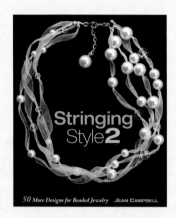

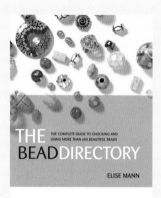